# FROM PAIN TO AWAKENING EVOLVING INTO WOMEN OF SUBSTANCE

Ahmadi

Copyright © 2011 by Ahmadi

*From Pain to Awakening: Evolving Into Women of Substance*
*Poems to Inform and Empower*
by Ahmadi

Printed in the United States of America

ISBN 9781613792193

All rights reserved solely by the author. The author guarantees all contents are original and do not infringe upon the legal rights of any other person or work. No part of this book may be reproduced in any form without the permission of the author. The views expressed in this book are not necessarily those of the publisher.

www.xulonpress.com

Ahmadu

7/22/11

Rina, Best Wishes as you evolved into a woman of substance —
God bless you alway
Fr Julie ☺

# Table of Contents

*From Pain to Awakening: Evolving Into Women of Substance*

# Foreword

We as women are a peculiar mixture of past, present, and future experiences. Hopefully, through each one, we learn and grow. If we grow, we come into a new awakening. One of being a more informed person from lessons learned. Some experiences in our lives have caused us pain as well as joy, and as certain as night follows day, they will continue to do so. Each of us must confront and overcome obstacles that cross our path.

It's said it takes a village of support to make us a person who is mentally, physically, emotionally, and spiritually whole. This village is comprised of spiritual mentors, family, strangers, friends, health professionals, and many other human anchors that often help us to stay afloat to not sink.

They may provide a smile, an encouraging word, a conversation that instills in us the determination to be proactive rather than withdraw from painful situations that hold us hostage. A hug when we need a comforting embrace, a phone call at the time we most need it, an unexpected and welcomed financial gift when we don't know how we are going to make it. A prayer that will bless and carry us through a most troublesome time, a song that will lift our spirit, a thoughtful present that will surprise us, an inspiring passage that will light an emotional spark within and make us think, a reflection on a life that allows us to know we aren't the only one in a trying situation. A silly joke that causes us to laugh, for laughter is a great healer, and many other positive moments to carry us through difficult times.

*From Pain to Awakening: Evolving Into Women of Substance*

We own the responsibility to ourselves to think right, listen right, speak right, act right, stand after falling, and have the courage to keep moving forward, even when it is the hardest thing to do.

I am truly thankful to the many people who have entered my life. For each experience, whether good or bad, has benefitted me.

These poems are a poetic mix of contemporary life stories many girls and women can relate. Boys and men can also identify with these stories. They explore themes of female identity and self-worth, a range of real-life family dynamics, health, race relations/diversity, and spirituality. These diverse reflections will kindle within you a distinct memory of the thoughts, feelings, and situations you or someone you know has encountered. They are intended to be thought provoking echoes. They hopefully will ignite an instinctive response within you to cast aside self-limiting behaviors, personally claim empowering ones, be eternally grateful for life situations you've overcome, and be inspired to make a difference in your life, someone you know, or take responsible action to move from pain to purpose to improve a human condition that can make a difference to many.

This range of empowerment poetry, factoids, relevant resources, talking point questions, Behavior Prevention/Change Model for Empowerment is written primarily for girls and women with universal relevance to boys, girls, women, and men. The talking point questions can be used for self-examination, 1 on 1 discussions, and group dialogue. The information can assist many to begin substantive critical thinking, sound decision making, and perseverance through perplexing life situations. The Behavior Prevention/Change Empowerment Model is a tool to be used to develop a plan for behavior prevention or change.

This book is beneficial to parents, grandparents, friends, teachers, counselors, coaches, and many others. It is for those who work in health, mental health, social services, education, criminal justice, and youth services.

Creative illustrations that captures the meaning of many of the poems are by the author's 13 and 11 year old granddaughters—evolving "young women of substance".

Always remember, there is a rainbow after every storm!

Peace and Blessings
Ahmadi

# Introduction

This book is a collection of poetry for girls and women to inform and empower them to be in control of themselves in relationships, in their sexual and reproductive lives, and in various life situations which can balance and imbalance their lives.

This book calls upon girls and women to become **AWARE, WILLING, AND INTERESTED** to **CHANGE** behaviors that don't **EMPOWER** them and **REJOICE** in overcoming disempowering behaviors. It challenges girls and women to continue to use that knowledge in a positive way for themselves and others.

It is for those who **THINK, FEEL, SAY** and have **SAID:**

I wish I could look like
I'm too fat—I'll go on a diet when
He abused me—I'm afraid he'll kill me if I leave (PhD professional woman)
I haven't dealt with past abuse BECAUSE
She was drunk—walking in traffic (mother of a co-ed)
I should leave him—What do you think? (an abused woman)
I can't believe he wants a paternity test
Can you tell me if you can have a DNA test on the baby while pregnant?
No I don't have a GED or HS diploma—I stopped school when I got pregnant
This will be my last time coming to jail
I hate this damn disease—family member of an Alzheimer's relative

*From Pain to Awakening: Evolving Into Women of Substance*

We're not together anymore—I don't care about him — (Pregnant teen/adult)
I know he/she doesn't have HIV/AIDS
She took my man—I'm going to make her regret it
Don't tell me how much to drink
My children don't like him BUT
I know my child needs a mentor BUT
I know he's married BUT
I just **HAVE** to buy this
How will I ever get over him
I just feel like ending my life
I don't like people from that race BECAUSE
I know drugs are messing up my life BUT
I'll stop smoking WHEN
I love him even though he treats me bad BECAUSE
I can't ask him to use condoms BECAUSE
I'm going to get my life together WHEN
We're in a monogamous relationship—I don't need any protection
Breastfeeding is GROSS
I deserve much better than the life I was living
I know he's gay BUT
A lot of middle school girls at my school are having sex and several freshmen are pregnant
When younger, I thought I **had** to be chosen by a man
She's 14 and wants to have a baby
I've learned to become a better parent
I had problems, my friends at school had problems—we were using each other to share problems
I believed I wasn't pretty— I hurt bad, and chose the wrong ones to fit in
I just can't take care of her and the baby she's having (distraught mother of a teen)
Is there a payment plan for obtaining an abortion?
I've learned to let go of anger
I've learned to respect myself more

# Dedication

This book is dedicated to the universal sisterhood of girls and women who are still transforming, non-conforming, and more to be. You are bold, classy, driven, and sassy! You may fall but you will rise! You may be shaken by past hurts but continue to try. Keep your mind free and not imprisoned. Know you can turn your life's pages! Hold your head high as you walk your individual path to be a *Woman of Substance!*

# Acknowledgements

It is with much gratitude that I thank my family, friends, colleagues at UVA Health System, and many other supportive ones who have given so much to me in my endeavor to write and publish this book. There are those who provided a listening ear, encouragement, individual talents, photography permissions, endorsements, marketing recommendations, prayers, speaking opportunities, and more. I truly am amazed and can attest that for whatever you want to do, if you take the first step there will be people who are placed in your path to help you make the next steps on your journey.

    I thank Al Leichter for the very informative Writing & Publishing Class he taught that I attended and the invaluable consultation he provided to me. I'm indebted to a friend who is no longer here but I know is looking down and wishing me well—Fred Freeman. Fred was the epitome of what any person would want in a friend. He was a former Assistant Editor for a major magazine and was the first one to look at my written work and tell me that with time, work, and dedication I could do what I am doing today. I am most grateful for the first editing of this book by my good friend Nadine Chase. She provided very valuable recommendations that were added. I thank Sandy Allen for the first reading and telling me that she could identify and knew it would resonate with many other women. I appreciate the informative consultation provided by Jody Sweeney, LCSW of UVA Health System.

*From Pain to Awakening: Evolving Into Women of Substance*

I truly thank Jessica Venable for her patience and superb Empowerment Model she designed from the information I provided. Her design captures exactly what I want to convey!

I thank Dr. Carlo C. DiClemente and the Guilford Press for allowing me to cite his Stages of Change in my Model for Self-Empowerment and Behavior Change.

I sincerely thank Vanessa Battle and Ron Barnabei of the Charlottesville/Albemarle County Jail who provided the volunteer forum for me to conduct my first and subsequent *Women of Substance* groups which are based on material from the book. Additionally, I want to thank a very wonderful and brilliant young woman, Jessica Strang who is pursuing her graduate education in the field of Psychology. She co-leads the groups at the jail with me and has been a wonderful complement to our group. I know she will be an outstanding Clinical Psychologist! I also am indebted to our first women's group who participated in September, 2010 and the interest they showed in my work with the group format provided to them. I thank them for the personal sharing of their lives which benefitted me more than words can say.

I thank my three granddaughters—Mariyah, Niara, and Tatiana for the many hours they assisted me in drawing the illustrations for this book. Their illustrations truly personify that "a picture is worth a thousand words".

I thank my sister Christine who has been more than I could ever expect in a sister and friend. She has been my most cherished supporter in all that I do. We talk every day and she frequently inquired on the status of the book and would often say "I better let you get back to your book".

I thank my daughter Jemila for her invaluable computer skills, recommendations, and editorial comments. Much gratitude to the UVA Teen Health Clinic's Outreach Program Educator, Mary Sullivan M.ED and DyanAretakis, FNP and Project Director of the Clinic for sponsoring me in the 2011 Charlottesville Festival of the Book. All of the staff at the Teen Clinic are the greatest!

I thank my other sponsors, Jennie Shuklis, MBA— Executive Director of the Focus Women's Resource Center and her marvelous staff. Additionally, James Pierce, Executive Director of the Cherry Avenue Boys and Girls Club and his very supportive staff!

I thank Anna DeLong, LCSW a colleague in the UVA Social Work Department. She initiated the first public reading of my work at UVA Health System. I appreciate my social work colleagues and co-workers from the PCC Women's Place Clinic who came to support me. They all are a fantastic group! I also thank Makeba Robinson, Program Director of the Booker T. Washington/Boys & Girls Club for inviting me to present at the April 2011 All Girls Conference in Staunton.

And above all, I thank my Creator for His sustaining presence in my life!

# Endorsements

*A**hmadi's wealth of experience in the field of women's health and her ability to connect with women and families enables her to write in a voice that will be immediately understood and absorbed. She tackles complex, even sensitive issues that are of great concern in today's society and makes it O.K. to think about them and talk about them in a new way. Her innovative method of raising awareness and empowering women should be on everyone's radar and in every middle school and high school curriculum!*

**Ann L. Kellams, M.D. IBCLC, FAAP**
**Medical Director, Newborn Nursery**
**Co-Director, The Healer's Art at UVA**
**American Academy of Pediatrics, Virginia Chapter**
**Co-Breastfeeding Coordinator, Education Committee**
**Assistant Professor, Department of Pediatrics**
**Faculty, Center for Biomedical Ethics and Humanities**
**UVA Health System**

*As a Transitional Coordinator for women in incarceration, I have seen the motivation that Ahmadi's work has provided to offenders in preparation for release. Her range of real life contemporary issues in her empowerment poetry allows offenders to think about themselves as individuals and empowers them to make choices as a result of their changed behaviors. Her work continues to be beneficial to transitional offenders as they successfully position themselves back into society.*

**Ron Barnabei,**
**Transitional Coordinator at Albemarle/Charlottesville Regional Jail**

*Wow! Congratulations Ahmadi on such powerful, meaningful, inspiring, creative, raw, honest work!*

**Anna DeLong, LCSW**
**Social Work Supervisor**
**UVA Health System**

*Never has the time been more urgent nor the message so clear for self-knowledge, personal responsibility, and life lessons!*

**Marilyn Pace, MA, RN, NE-BC**
**Ambulatory Manager of Women's Health**
**University of Virginia Health System**

# UNAWARENENESS

## Female Identity and Self Worth

*From Pain to Awakening: Evolving Into Women of Substance*

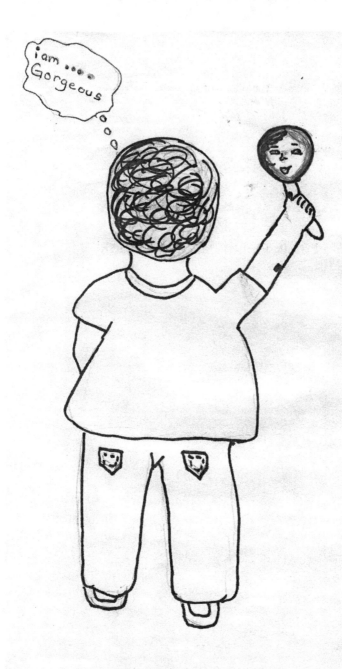

**Do you know?**

Real Girls, Real Pressure: A National Report on the State of Self-Esteem

Commissioned: June 2008 71% of girls with low self-esteem feel their appearance does not measure up, including not feeling pretty enough, thin enough or stylish or trendy enough (compared to 29% of girls with high self-esteem)[1]

78% of girls with low self-esteem admit that it is hard to feel good in school when you do not feel good about how you look (compared to 54% of girls with high self-esteem). [1]

75% of teenage girls felt "depressed, guilty, and shameful" after spending just three minutes leafing through a fashion magazine.[1]

62% of all girls feel insecure or not sure of themselves.[1]

75% of girls with low self-esteem reported engaging in negative activities such as disordered eating, cutting, bullying, smoking, or drinking when feeling bad (compared to 4% of girls with high self-esteem).[1]

# BODY IMAGE
Inside Out—Outside In
It Is All About You

Your nose may be flat, wide, or narrow
Your teeth may have a gap that highlights a distinctive smile
Your hair may be straight, curly, or most unruly
Your skin may be white, bright, caramel, or darker than night
Your bust size may be 30 to 65 inches plus
Your hips may be the same size and make you cuss
Your legs may be long, short, or bow
Your feet may fit shoe size 10 and continue to grow
Your weight may be 99 pounds wet or exceed the scales highest number
What's most important to always remember
Have positive feelings about yourself on the inside
To accept who you are on the outside
You determine what's important to you!
Change occurs when you decide what you want to do
And what you will change
Not what others tell you to rearrange
To become the vision of how you want to be on the outside
Must first come from what has changed in you on the inside


## TALKING POINT QUESTIONS

How do you define "self-esteem?"

How do you feel good about the "body" you are wrapped in?

Why is the "inner you" more important than the "outer you?

Why is it important to not let others make you feel inadequate?

**Do you know?**

7 in 10 girls believe they are not good enough or do not measure up in some way, including their looks, performance in school and relationships with friends and family.[1]

**Resource:** http://www.girlshealth.gov[2] A great government self-esteem website with interactive games, quizzes, and useful information for young girls, teens, and parents.

**Resource:** For leadership, education, training, support, resources, advocacy, information in supporting healthy youth and young families: **http://www.healthyteennetwork.org/**[3]

## (SONG)
# MORE THAN THE OUTSIDE

There's more to you than the Outside
There's more to you than the Outside
Believe in yourself—Hold your head high
Believe in yourself—Hold your head high
It takes time to learn this and not deny
There's more to you than on the outside
Forget about words people say that make you cry
Forget about words people say that make you cry
Sometimes you'll feel lost and hurt inside
Believe in yourself—It's OK to cry
Believe in yourself—It's OK to cry
It takes time to learn this and not deny
There's more to you than on the outside
Believe in yourself, hold your head high
Believe in yourself, hold your head high
There's an exceptional you on the inside
There's an exceptional you on the inside
Believe in yourself, hold your head high
Believe in yourself, hold your head high
There's more to you than the outside
There's an exceptional you on the inside!


## TALKING POINT QUESTIONS

Why is it important to not "get caught up" in how you look?

Why is it important to accentuate your good qualities and work on your challenging ones?

Why is it important to not let others set your trend and define who you are?

What actions can you take to have positive feelings about yourself?

*From Pain to Awakening: Evolving Into Women of Substance*

## Impressions
What do they really mean?

Impressions!
Impressions!

What do they really mean?
Take a look at what impresses you and think!
"Does what impress me mean anything?"

You're impressed you have a man who pays part of your rent
What happens when he drops out of sight and rent is due next week?

You're impressed he leases the latest luxury car
How does this fit into who you are?

You're impressed he gives you his Visa card for a designer purse
What happens when you find out you're not the first!

When you're in touch with who you are
You will know this thinking won't take you far


**TALKING POINT QUESTIONS**

How do we get "caught up" in meaningless impressions?

Why is it necessary to get in touch with yourself to know the real and false beliefs you have?

Can buying "things" to make you happy or to "impress" others make you happy?

## Think Then Act

Act then Think
Or
Think then Act

Remember this rhyme to keep on track
Think before you Act—There's less impact

Act then Think
Don't be surprised when you're led astray
When you ignore advice & experiences that come your way!

If the ultimate price becomes colors you wear that are orange, red, and stripes
And you're surrounded by various "behavior types"

Who are you impressing?
When you are now stressing
And trying to work out the unlearned lesson!


## TALKING POINT QUESTIONS

How can impulsive behavior affect you?

How can it effect those you're close to (family, friends)?

What can you do to stop impulsive behaviors?

What resources/people can you ask for help?

**Do you know?**

**<u>Bullying Statistics:</u>**

Children who are bullied are more at risk to be depressed, lonely, anxious, have low self-esteem, feel sick, and contemplate suicide. [4]

5.4 percent of high school students (about 864,000) report staying home at least one day a month because they fear for their safety.[5]

**<u>Importance of Compassion—Definition:</u>**

Deep awareness of the suffering of another coupled with the wish to relieve it.[6]

**It is my belief** compassion begins at home. It is how we show respect, concern, love, and understanding to those who are a part of our family and solving differences peacefully and respectfully. It is important to role model this behavior so that there is a benchmark on how to show compassion within and outside of the family.

**Resources:**

**gethelp@nvc.org[7] 1 800 FYI-CALL**

**stopbullyingnow.hrsa.gov/kids[8]**

**www.bully.org[9]**

The Trevor Helpline: Specializing in gay and lesbian youth suicide prevention. 1 800 850-8078

## The Camera Is Rolling

I've been in the presence of girls and women of different colors and ages
Treating each other with total disrespect
I think—Do they understand their uncontrollable rages?

No concern how they represent!
Not a clue to their run away behavior

The taunting, critical looks
The stares of contempt from head to toe
The threatening moves
The mean slights without caring how they make others feel
The in your face attitude
The cold and cynical words said to cut deep
The lack of sensitivity to the effect they will reap
The limited sense of the girl or woman they believe they are
As they lower their self-respect bar
Twisted beliefs on fighting to hold a **boy-man**
Not realizing that when he became involved with someone else
He was part of the plan

It takes two to decide when and where to meet
Yet they solely blame "the other female" for the shared love secret

They cause situations like this and other trite behavior
They never thought to turn the video camera on themselves for a better view
And watch their X-rated scenes preview

Girls and women will rise to a higher level of self-respect
When they can watch what their image projects

Sit down and assess their ways
And truly be aware what their image displays

A girl or woman who has true awareness
Will not run, flee, or joke about negative self-portrayal
But look with a critical eye
The changes needed she can't deny

Be aware how you direct the images of your life
A girl or woman with self-respect is aware of her presence
She represents her best—and shuns behavior that makes others feel meaningless

## TALKING POINT QUESTIONS

Why is self-examination important?

How do you define compassion and empathy?

Why is it important to have compassion and empathy as part of your character?

What reward comes from being jealous?

What do you gain by being mean to someone?

How do you define bullying?

How does bullying affect the victim?

How does it affect the bully?

What causes some girls and women to physically/verbally attack or "hate on" other girls/women?

Why is it important to seek family, friends, or professional support to help you eliminate negative behavior?

# Last Night

Last night I didn't pray
Disillusioned—I screamed at the darkness—"Go Away"!
It's funny because it continued to stay
It laughed at me
It mocked me
It became darker and darker
It controlled me!
It didn't console me
It tested me!
Arrested me!

I was confused, angry, and hurt by words said yesterday
I tried to forget and wanted to see the light of a new day
I wanted the cruel words to not replay

The night surrendered to a new day
When I got down on my knees and prayed

### TALKING POINT QUESTIONS

Why is it important to not let anyone control your emotions?

If they do, how will it affect you?

How can prayer, meditation, affirmations, talking to a support source you trust help you?

Why is holding in your anger harmful to you?

Why is it important to let it go?

## Diamond

You're a Diamond and More!
Accept compliments on how you look
And be wise to know looks aren't a hook!

It's more to you than what's seen from the outside
The value of who you are
Is the appraisal you assign to your self-worth

Work on yourself with the dedication Michelangelo had to the Sistine Chapel
Possess dignity and tenacity like Fannie Lou Hamer

Speak your words with the articulation of Barbara Jordan
Stand against sexual disrespect like Anita Hill

Be a woman of many talents like Maya Angelou
Stay committed to your goals like Hillary Clinton

Set your dreams high like Supreme Court Justice Sonia Sotomayor
Design a monumental edifice like Maya Lin

Work to save the environment like Dr Wangari Maathai!
Craft your talents and defy the odds like Butterfly McQueen, Moninque, and Jennifer Hudson

Blaze a trail of excellence like Oprah Winfrey
Possess the compassion and strength of Mother Teresa

Excel in science and multiple languages like astronaut Dr. Mae Jemison
Uplift your country and your ideals like Golda Meir and Indira Ghandi

Express your creativity like Judith Jamison!
Examine right and wrong and act against social injustice like Rosa Parks

Be "unbought and unbossed" like Shirley Chisholm
Show the world you are multi-dimensional like Ellen Degeneres!

Be a woman in her own right like Coretta Scott-King, Michelle Obama, and Princess Diana
Desire to do what's right like many women you'll never meet

Who aren't on walls of fame but daily do great feats
Develop the depth within

So the quality of who you are
Is more precious than the rarest Diamond or the most distant Star!

# RELATIONSHIPS

## Looking for Love in All the Wrong Places

There are times in women's lives when they fill in empty spaces of their lives with a relationship they believe will close spaces of fear, loneliness, shaky self-confidence, rejection, boredom, hurt and other feelings not given serious thought. These moments occur in single as well as married women's lives.

It's also true for many women without a "love" relationship, whether for short or long periods of time, to fall into a pattern of entering another relationship too soon because of the desire to have the caring, attention, intimacy, and feelings of being "connected". When the relationship does not work out with that man, many times become obsessive and try to win him back, even when he wasn't that loving, caring, or faithful. Some women obsess when the relationship ends, lose sleep, become anxious and resentful. Some try to conveniently be in places they think their men will go or call their cell and home phones continuously. Some take it to more out of control extremes resulting in harassment, physical harm and even homicide. There are other women who count their losses and wait for the next relationship to emotionally re-charge them, and others who learn from past troubling experiences to be cautious to not repeat them.

Statistics reflect that as women, we will outlive men and will spend a portion of our lives alone. It's a reality we all must face. It is important for each woman to accept herself and her insecurities. It is important to feel comfortable discovering who we are and where our challenges and strengths lie. What harm is there to take the time to sit with oneself for personal reflection. To discover what truly makes you happy, what motivates your spirit. What makes you laugh, what makes you cry, what stirs anger within, and what calms your spirit.

*From Pain to Awakening: Evolving Into Women of Substance*

Reflect on the emotions, impulses, and actions that lead you into relationships and what occurs to cause them to end or to continue when they should have ended. Think about what makes you hold on when you need to let go. Think of the times you ignored friends, family, and personal interests and became so involved that you lost your own identity, what you enjoyed, and what was important to you.

The following poems express various ways women come into relationships and the thoughts and choices to be made before entering a relationship and how to decide it is time to end one that is painful and damaging.

# WHEN HE LOVES ME

When he loves me and its for real
He takes time to work out the complexities a relationship gives
When he loves me and its for real
Its oh So Sweet!
Its like endless days of chocolate treats!
When he loves me and its for real
I feel his presence whether far or near
When he loves me and its for real
In his presence I have no fear!
When he loves me and its for real
Respect and love is his will
When he loves me and its for real
He holds me like a precious jewel and his love I feel!
When he loves me and its right
We can talk forever into the night
When he loves me and its tight
Misunderstandings that come are worked out right
When he loves me its all good!
Because he loves me in all the ways a real man should!


## TALKING POINT QUESTIONS

What behaviors let you know a man loves you?

What behaviors let you know a man doesn't love you?

*From Pain to Awakening: Evolving Into Women of Substance*

## QUALITIES

I asked her
Have you thought of qualities in a male to explore?
Do you know your standards before he knocks at your door?
No she said, that sounds a bit like a chore!

I said, I know this sounds like an oddity
However, let's talk reality

Females of different ages make mistakes at various stages
When they fail to determine qualities for their *male standards* list

Let's begin with **Respect** a key foundation
Followed by **Trust** an important part of the equation

**Positive Behavior** and **Financially Stable**
**Interested in Life** beyond the cable

**Mature Character** when problems arise
**Ready to Communicate** and work out differences that come your way
**Willing to Compromise** when decisions must be made

**Thoughtful to Listen** and not guided by Rumors
Often **Funny** with a **Good Sense of Humor**

**Commitment** to one another you wouldn't trade

These are some Qualities to have on your list
Be a **Woman of Substance**-No Matter Your Age
Be deliberate and in the know
About who can enter your life
AND
    WHO
        MUST
            GO!

## TALKING POINT QUESTIONS

Why is it important for girls and women to have a males standards list?

Think about the male qualities in this poem—are there more?

What additional qualities would you add?

How does the saying "if you don't stand for something, you'll fall for anything" apply to having standards in a relationship?

By Tatiana E.

## Like A Candy Bar On A Shelf

Why sit like a candy bar on a shelf?"
Waiting for him to select you for himself

When he comes with his swag
Be aware of some of the unpredictability in his bag

He may say you're most appealing
And three months later say—"Oh—by the way—I've got someone else with whom I'm Chilling"!

"Why sit like a candy bar on a shelf?"
Now thinking no one will select you for yourself

Feeling blue and wondering—"How did it come to this?"
Sit with yourself and reflect—"What did I miss?"

"Why did I sit like a candy bar on a shelf?"
Waiting to be chosen with little understanding of myself

"Why did I trust that the relationship would last forever?"
And be unaware that relationships can crumble like dry leaves in fall weather

"Why didn't I know the type of qualities I wanted in a man??
"Or did I think that was passe!"
"And I didn't need any rules to play."

Time, reflection, and standards I set for myself
Will keep me from sitting like a candy bar on a shelf!"


### TALKING POINT QUESTIONS

What causes girls and women to be "like candy bars on a shelf?"

*From Pain to Awakening: Evolving Into Women of Substance*

What role does society play in devaluing girls and women?

What role does television, media advertising, movies, music videos, magazines, etc. play in devaluing girls and women?

Do you believe this is an area of concern and action?

How would you inform a girl or woman on this issue? (ex. Sister, niece, daughter, friend)?

How would you inform a boy or man on this issue? (ex. Brother, nephew, son, friend)?

# THINK, CONTEMPLATE
## Quick decisions can cause long-term heartache

Careful decision making is required on the person with whom you will date
This is serious and not to be taken lightly and be guided by "I know" and "What ifs"

**I know** he's sweet and kind,
Our time is short but I want him to be mine
**I know** he's someone I can build my life around

What if we haven't known each other long
**I know** we're good for each other

What could possibly go wrong?

**I know** our love will last,
Don't worry about me
Please don't bother!

What if he has a temper!

**I know** he's for real when he says his last love made him that way
**I know** I can soothe his hurt and make it go away!

**I know** I can change his feelings of rejection and cruel words he says

What if he speaks harsh, loves me one minute, and acts cold without warning
**I know** if I give him love and ignore these minor actions, he will be different by morning

**I know** he drinks and gets moody quick
I believe him when he says he'll quit

**I know** he has some legal issues and behaviors to correct
You just don't understand, we really connect!

**I know** I can change his ways
**I know** he can be kind, loving, and not crazy

The **I knows** and **what ifs** are emotional defenses to set your life off course
As women, we often fail to make the best decisions about the men to be in our future
And take lightly how they will accept responsibility if we become pregnant

**Think, Contemplate** about who will be a part of your life
When you rush into relationships quickly **or** become pregnant too fast
The repercussions can be a lifetime and difficult to correct!

## TALKING POINT QUESTIONS

What causes girls and women to think much too soon about commitment?

Why is it important to take time to develop a relationship?

How important is it to be friends first? Why?

## SEARCHING FOR LOVE

You may not have had a father to tuck you in at Night
Or
Checked closets before you went to sleep to calm your fright
A thousand apologies will never make it right
What I want to share—and shed some light
Don't look to boys or men to hold you tight and make you believe all will be right
Their hugs and promises of love aren't true expressions of the tenderness you seek
The empty space in your heart you want to fill
Can't be replaced by shallow encounters that leaves your soul chilled
This will affect your self-respect
Leaving you feeling lost—Needing a reality check
Stop! Know this isn't you
Losing yourself in misguided "love"
Deprives you of the real love and respect you deserve
Wake up! This isn't you!
Begin to believe in you and work on hurt you can't run from or hide
Work to overcome feelings of rejection
To have self-respect to start your life in a new direction!


## TALKING POINT QUESTIONS

Can a male "love interest" be a replacement for an absent father?

What causes girls/women to seek love in the wrong places?

What do they need to do to stop looking in the wrong places?

Do you have to justify why your father is not in your life?

What personal qualities do you need to have and/or develop to deal with his absence?

Can you "survive" and "overcome" without an involved father in your life?

# MAKING LOVE OR BEING LOVED

Being held in an erotic embrace
With the veil of darkness hiding his and your face
Can make you believe
Love is ruling in this place!
Is making love and being loved the same?
You may argue, "Why does this question have to be asked?"
Are you insane?
Why spread doubt and take what is simple to a higher plane?
It has no need to be explained!

It's most peculiar how they're believed to be the same
And given identical equality in the relationship game
**Making Love** can be calculating
Based upon emotions with little depth and relating
**Being Loved** is liberating and worthy of celebrating!
It's getting to know each other and who you are
What you like and what you desire
Being real and compassionate with the words you speak
And allowing time to take you to a quality of love
Worth the time and work to make complete
**Making Love** or **Being Loved**
Which one is the most important that you seek?


## TALKING POINT QUESTIONS

How does having sex get confused with having love?

Why is it important to have a clear understanding of the differences?

Why is it "smart" to value yourself and not offer your body as a token to solidify a relationship?

*From Pain to Awakening: Evolving Into Women of Substance*

*From Pain to Awakening: Evolving Into Women of Substance*

# I WANT A MAN
## Reality vs Fantasy

You say you want a man to wine and dine you at a candle lit table
Are you aware of the real you to be
And not live a storybook fantasy
A real man wants a woman who is his equal
Not one who sits for hours watching a Lifetime sequel
A real man wants a woman who can converse on many topics
Not one who gets jealous and searches his pants pockets
A real man wants a woman who is independent with her career on course
Not one who is contemplating her next nail color choice
A real man wants a woman who is confident
Not one who wonders—"Can he pay my rent?"
A real man wants a woman who can discuss a presidential caucus debate
Not one who is anxious for the next dinner date
A real man wants a woman who won't set a trap
To rope him into an unwanted marriage
And says—
That's a wrap!
Think with an honest and open mind
About the real woman to be
And the girl to leave behind!


**TALKING POINT QUESTIONS**

What do you think about the expectation "wants" of the man in this poem?

Is it important for men to have standards for the women they want in their lives?

Are the standards in this poem realistic?

*From Pain to Awakening: Evolving Into Women of Substance*

## COMMITMENT TOO SOON
### What Was I Thinking

Why is it that when he takes me out several times on a date
Wheels in my head spin and I begin to elaborate
We seem like a good twosome—He could be a great mate!
Thoughts of commitment begin to peak
I have to put on my emotional brakes—Squeak! Squeak!
Take a deep breath—aaahh— And regroup
Moving too fast can put you in an emotional loop
I talk to sister friends about this revelation
Many respond with wise interpretations

They say as women we move too fast
They say know as much of his present and a lot of his past

Get to know friends from his graduation class
See if he was Rude or a bit Crass
See how he treats his mother—Is it with Class?
If he treats her well and with respect
That's a sign he might Pass!

It says he has standards and is no fool!

Keep emotions under control
Don't readily share your body or your soul

Does he have a clear police record?
Is he absent from the offender register?
Can he have an intelligent conversation?
Does he have a bank account? At least at one location!

If he fails this test
Do I really have to tell you what's best?

## TALKING POINT QUESTIONS

What causes girls and women to think much too soon about commitment?

Why is it important to take time to develop a relationship?

How important is it to be friends first? Why?

*From Pain to Awakening: Evolving Into Women of Substance*

# I GOT A MAN
## Flashbacks from Reality TV

I turn on the television to watch the news
The first vision I see is women with lots of attitude
I watch and listen to their feud
Embarrassed for them that they could care less who sees their mood
I marvel at the nerve it must take
To be seen by millions looking like a bad B-Movie remake
PLEASE! Give me a break!

AT LEAST I'VE GOT A MAN
Becomes one woman's repeated chorus
It went something like this, until she became hoarse
He may have been with you last night
Held you tight
Fixed your cracked mini-van light
Just remember this
He's mine, make no mistake
He lives with me and at least I've got a man

I know if he stays out late
He will be back, and I'll wait
Can't you see, At least I've got a man

I don't push him to pay bills
He pays what he can
The passion he gives is all I need
Don't you see, At least I've got a man

STOPPPPPPPPPPP!
Have you listened to yourself?
Can you open your mind to this nonsense chatter?
Step into reality, and Confront this matter!
He doesn't honor you with his rude behavior
Does he brag about you?
Or does he get tongue-tied—and hasn't a clue?

Does he pepper all of his comments with
AT LEAST I'VE GOT A WOMAN?
I don't think so!
You are a sacrificial lamb
On a sacrificial platter
You are just another woman
And to him
YOU REALLY DON'T MATTER!

**TALKING POINT QUESTIONS**

What occurs for some girls and women to accept males that are not good for them?

Where does a female's self-respect and confidence go when she is disrespected?

What responsibility do boys and men have for their behavior in relationships?

What responsibility do girls and women have for setting boundaries for male behavior in their relationships?

## From Pain to Awakening: Evolving Into Women of Substance

# THE OTHER WOMAN
## Invisible

So you say it's ok to be the "other woman"

Are you content with the love portions you're given
I know you laugh and say I'm tripping
And it's not my business the love portion you receive
You're right, You're on point, I do Agree!

Please believe I'm not trying to get your nose out-of-joint
Just looking from a different vantage point
Your view may be a bit out of focus
Due to being so close and thinking what I say is bogus

Statistics gives your status a two year average run
You may have claimed your status due to a limited pool of good men your age
Or society's pressure to be part of two and not one
Or maybe just out for a "little fun"

What becomes maddening to the title you take
Are the emotional highs and periodic heartache
The anticipated times are exciting and filled with intrigue
The love appreciated for what you receive
The lows do come and over time you begin to lose your view
And contemplate how your choice now limits you!
You feel so blue
You're angry about the portion of love you receive
And try to live with arrangements you did agree

You bargain with yourself there will be more
And anxiously await the knock at the door
Rehearsing to yourself again and again
There will be more!
Dreading feeling more like a puppet on a string
Your emotions bounce with frequent mood swings

Yet you eagerly wait for the telephone to ring
As you live with your portion, you wipe away tears with a bitter sting!

When a year turns into another
You begin to question—"Where is this relationship going?"
"Where is the me I once knew?"
You begin to think
"I can't take it no more!"
When the anxiety and pain becomes more than you can take
You know there's a decision to make
Control will return to you
You will STOP, Walk away, and be Visible again

## TALKING POINT QUESTIONS

What is the personal cost of being "invisible"?

What steps do you take to regain who you are and be visible again?

What if you don't want to be visible and are satisfied with your status?

How long can you be satisfied with this status?

## TRACKS OF MY TEARS

Be aware the day will come
When you'll feel lost without that special someone
The one you shared secrets and laughed the most

Tears will come at different times
You wipe them away as the clock loudly chimes

You pace the floor
Watching and waiting for his knock at the door
You search your mind as memories of past incidents unwind
You remember hurried goodbyes from his cell phone calls
You think, many times he did seem nervous
You felt uneasy, thinking there was something beneath the surface
His past calls were long with or without purpose
Now they're short and he acts so nervous!
He used to stay long and not rush
He then changed
Often saying he had business at home that couldn't wait
You then began to ruminate
You told yourself—"This can't be fate!"
Your eyes fluttered as you became fearful
Now you are nervous and shaky, feeling numb inside
Your thoughts want to scream, you just want to hide
You pace back and forth, as an actor on a stage
As you become more angry, like a lion in a cage

You want to call him to confirm if your suspicions are true
You want to be composed to not become unglued

You nervously call and say, "We must talk."
He says, "Ok", but first I have to take my dog Oscar for a walk."

He says, "What's this all about?"
You say, "Just come here." Trying to stay calm and not S — H — O — U— T!

When you hear the knock at the door
The anger returns as you walk swiftly across the floor

"What's going down?" He asks
A questioning look, with a guilt face mask
You don't want to know, but you have to ask

"Am I the only one you see?"
He denies it at first, but you know, and begin to face reality

"I'm sorry," he says, "I must come clean."
"I've been seeing someone—her name is Janine."

"I didn't mean for it to go down this way!"
You scream, cry, and yell—"Go away!"
It's so crazy because a part of you wants him to stay

The tears that form tracks on your face will dry and erase
Take time to heal and review the past
Treasure times that were a blast!

Talk with trusted friends to lift your mood
Nurture your soul with meditation and comfort food

Time is the best healer of pain
You will come full circle
And return to the you who is whole again

## TALKING POINT QUESTIONS

What can happen to your self-esteem when the relationship you're involved ends?

What can you do to get through this difficult time?

How can you continue to feel you matter when your relationship ends?

How do you take care of yourself?

How important are friends and family during this time?

How can friends and family be too helpful and too involved during this time?

How do you learn from this experience?

## ENDINGS

Unbreak My Heart
Vs.
I'm Nobody Until Somebody Loves Me

A deeply regretful woman in a love song pleads with her former lover to
"unbreak" her heart
She begs him to return to undo the hurt when he walked out of her life

Another classic song falsely moans
A woman is "nobody" without someone to love her

Many women can feel this to be their emotional condition
When the love relationship they're in comes to an ending

Like snow that melts on a window pane
Like seasons that end and will come again
Like laughter that is spontaneous and then fades

Relationships have beginnings and endings
Often gone before they're made

Some grow and evolve
Some lose momentum and dissolve

The pain of the ending can hurt and prolong
If you don't take care and work to be strong

Through this evolution
Your mind and body feel like they're in a revolution

Take heed to your emotions
So tears don't become oceans

Acknowledge with renewed confidence
And much insistence

"I am somebody when there is no one to love me."

Say this without resistance!
Say this again and again
With much Persistence!
Until a renewed you returns with a calm resilience

## I TRUSTED YOU

I trusted you
I Believed What You Said
I shouldn't have given to you what was mine instead
Now I'm feeling "dissed"!
A better term for what I'm feeling is "pissed"!
Because you now act like I don't exist

I listened to you and believed I mattered
Now I'm feeling used
I know how I'm feeling—and I'm not confused!

I'm putting you on BLAST!
I'm hurting now—but it's not going to LAST!

If finding me means losing you
I'm glad I found me while losing you!

*From Pain to Awakening: Evolving Into Women of Substance*

# FINANCES
## Wants vs Needs

Know your wants from your needs
Don't prioritize designer labels as necessities

Dress with taste and discretion
Forget about those you want to create an impression

Shop and purchase in moderation
Don't leave your finances in annihilation

Know how to determine what comes first
And what waits 'til last

Work, save, and invest your money
Being broke isn't funny
The friends you had when you were on a roll
Know when you don't have money
And can become distant and cold

Take a guess on friends who will stick around
When you're in a financial meltdown!


## TALKING POINT QUESTIONS

Why is it important to know the difference between wants and needs?

Why is money management important?

How can wise money management help you now and in the future?

Why is it important to learn about financial management from childhood thru adulthood?

**Do you know?**

Practical information for children and parents to learn money management skills. Fun, free, educational money management games and more!
**http:www.practicalmoneyskills.com/personalfinances/creditdebt/**[10]

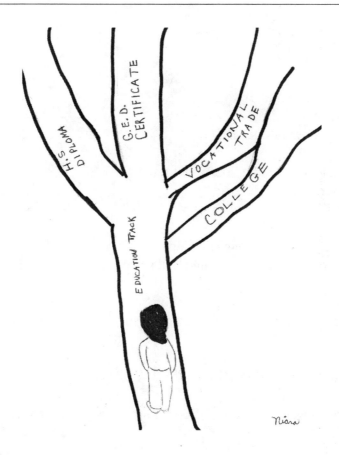

## Do you know?

Every school day, more than seven thousand students become dropouts. Annually, that adds up to about 1.3 million students who will not graduate from high school with their peers.[11]

The average annual income for a high school dropout in 2005 was $17,299, compared to $26,933 for a high school graduate.[11]

The crisis is neither silent nor invisible, one in three high school students do not graduaate.[12]

12 percent of the nation's high schools produce nearly half of the nation's dropouts.[12]

# EDUCATION
Educate or Vegetate

Develop your mind everyday
Stay in school
Go back or get on the GED track

Decide on college or a vocational trade
Life is serious
There will be time for play

Read, learn, expand your knowledge
Be able to converse on international trade and the political page

Use your mind as a strategic weapon
Command your thoughts and slay ignorance to release your potential


## TALKING POINT QUESTIONS

Were you aware of the US dropout statistics? What do you think about them?

How will limited education affect a person's life?

Why are educational goals and good study habits important?

Why is reading important?

Why is it important to be selective in television viewing?

Why is it important to complete high school or get a GED?

Why is it important to further your education as far as you can and never stop learning?

## DUMBING DOWN

Don't be ashamed of your intellect!
When those around want you to dumb down
And go on an endless merry-go-round
Excel to a higher ground!
You will attract others like you who are around
Who won't limit their future when someone puts them down!

## TALKING POINT QUESTIONS

What does it mean to be an "independent" thinker?

Why is it important to be an independent thinker?

Why is it important to be a leader when confronted with negative choices?

Why is it important to weigh the good and bad of situations that are potentially harmful to you?

What habits have you developed to achieve?

What habits have you developed to underachieve?

How do you work on the underachieving habits?

Do you know resources to help you excel?

What is your responsibility to achieve?

# HEALTH AND WELLNESS

**Do you know?**

The prevalence of adults in the U.S. who are obese is still high, with about one-third of adults obese in 2007-2008.[13]

In 2006, 631,636 people died of heart disease. It caused 26% of deaths—more than one in every four—in the U.S. Half of the deaths to heart disease were women. Risk factors: tobacco use, diets high in saturated fat, physical inactivity, obesity, alcohol. [14]

Childhood obesity has more than tripled in the past 30 years. The prevalence of obesity among children aged 6 to 11 years increased from 6.5% in 1980 to 19.6% in 2008. The prevalence of obesity among adolescents aged 12 to 19 years increased from 5.0% to 18.1%. [15]

Babies born to obese women are almost three times as likely to die within one month of birth and almost twice as likely to be stillborn than babies born to women of normal weight. [16]

## SO WHAT—THE FOOD BATTLE

**So what** if I salt food before I taste
**So what** if I'm out of breath walking a fast pace

**So what** if I put mounds of sugar in coffee and fruit punch drinks

**So what** if I pinch more than an inch and can't bend to tie a shoe lace
**So what** if I smoke cigarettes like I'm in a smoke race

**So what** if I want burgers and fries
And at yearly physicals tell my doctor little white lies

**So what** if I eat cookies and sugary foods
Oh how white chocolate sets my mood!

Vegetables, lean meat, and whole grains are ok
I just don't have the desire to eat them every day!

**I know** I've got to do better
**I know** I'm in denial

**I know** my waist is hard to measure
**I know** good health is a treasure!

**I know** food choices and limited exercising is leading me to disaster!
**I know** my heart is overworked and pumping faster

Old habits are hard to break
I think of the discipline—it makes me shake!
**I know** this battle I must win—not fake!

## TALKING POINT QUESTIONS

Why is it important to have a well-balanced diet?

Why is exercise important?

How can obesity affect your health?

Why is it important to not eat while watching television?

Why is it important to be proactive in managing chronic health problems?

## SHARED PAIN WITH A FRIEND

Hurt revealed
Cold as a Chill
That tortuous invader I dismissed is back
I'm caught in a reality I again fear

The moisture in her red-rimmed eyes, the crack in her voice
The pain on her face
My heart quickened and my thoughts raced

She anxiously waited, yet feared the results
She felt uncertain and scared to guess
My heart heavy to see the pain she couldn't hide

"Why can't I change this?"
My thoughts screamed from inside

Why do the ones who do their best
Often endure the cruelest tests?

I want to strike this negative force with no face
I feel the hurt only time puts in its place

She provides more strength than I give
The grace she carries this burden is a testimony to her will not to break
And her strength to live despite heartache

We warmly embrace
This intruder is just another challenge we'll face
We'll crush it with attitude and a whole lot of faith!


**TALKING POINT QUESTIONS.**

Why is it important to be there for a friend or family member who is going through a health or other significant life challenge?

What are some ways to help them?

What are some ways to take care of you in the process of helping them?

## Do you know?

Dementia: Is characterized by the loss of or decline in memory and other cognitive abilities. It is caused by various diseases and conditions that result in damaged brain cells. [17]

Alzheimer's Disease: Most common type of dementia. Symptoms: Difficulty remembering names and recent events is often an early sign. Later symptoms include impaired judgment, disorientation, confusion, behavior changes and difficulty speaking, swallowing, and walking.[17]

Every 70 seconds, someone in America develops Alzheimer's disease. By mid-century, someone will develop Alzheimer's every 33 seconds. [17]

Vascular disease may be a particularly powerful factor in the prevalence of Alzheimer's among African -Americans. [18]

Data from a large-scale longitudinal study indicate that persons with a history of either high blood pressure or high cholesterol levels are twice as likely to get Alzheimer's disease. Those with both risk factors are four times as likely to become demented. The implication of these discoveries are enormous for African-Americans, among whom vascular disease and its factors are disproportionately present. [18]

# TIRED BRAIN

Quietly we walk at a slow pace
Different worries on our face
The day will come when she won't know my name or recognize my face

Who carries the fault?
Who carries the blame?

Why couldn't this memory robber stay hidden and not invade our space?
I will slowly lose my most special friend
Her past, present, and future will be stolen, We don't know when
We've held each other close and often sobbed

Who carries the fault?
Who carries the blame?

I will stand beside her all the way
I will gently let her know things she can't recall
Like when we laughed and climbed a rock wall!

I will do this with dignity and not to shame
We didn't ask for this journey but we'll take it amid the pain?


## TALKING POINT QUESTIONS

What is the difference between dementia and Alzheimer's disease?

How can we address this "unspoken" health crisis proactively?

How can you help relatives and friends with this health problem?

What support do you need as a friend or caregiver of someone with dementia?

By Mariyah

**Do you know?**

A randomized control group of college students demonstrated that a selected mind-body intervention, Transcendental Meditation, decreased psychological distress and increased coping in young adults at risk for hypertension.[19]

## YOUR TIME
Taking Care of You

Allow solitude to relax your mind
Let it be quiet without repetitious thought drills
Dismiss the world by closing your eyes
Slowly inhale and release tension inside
Center yourself so pressures don't collide

## TALKING POINT QUESTIONS

Why is it important to know what stress is and how to manage it?

Why is it important to your mental health to meditate or take "me time" for yourself?

Why is it important to not feel guilty about taking time for yourself?

## ROCKING TO THE RHYTHM

I'm rocking to the rhythm
Totally Living!
Taking time to not always be driven
Soothing myself with some Coltrane, Alicia Keyes, and Miles
Remembering good times with naughty smiles
Loving this time to truly unwind
Forgetting about today and leaving it behind!
Taking time to honor Me in My own special way
Yes! I'm rocking to the rhythm!

# PARENTING

## On Deciding To Be A Parent

Becoming a parent is a serious decision. It should be considered with thought, planning, and true understanding. Being a parent is a 24 hour job.

It's a lifetime experience that unfolds into different responsibilities as your child matures.

Many of the roles you will assume: doctor, nurse, counselor, mediator, negotiator, activities director, storyteller, chauffeur, teacher, friend, disciplinarian, spiritual mentor, meal planner, financial advisor, and more. You will be required to provide comfortable shelter, medical care, clothing, well-balanced meals and snacks, toileting and training until your child becomes independent, an abundance of love, supervision, moral and ethical instructions. You will also provide instruction on personal responsibility, fairness, tolerance, judgment, decision making, limit setting, social relationship skills, values, and more.

Know that parenting requires love, dedication, planning, and a great deal of understanding. Do not take this responsibility lightly. Be certain that when you make the decision to have a baby you are aware of the promise you will be making and the changes to your lifestyle that will occur.

To be responsible for assuming the awesome task of rearing an infant into a well-adjusted adult will require a great amount of work. The reward will be a satisfying one when you understand what the parenting job takes. It is the most serious commitment in life you'll ever make.

**Do you know?**

**The Boy's Town National Hotline** is a National Hotline that children and parents can call with any problem at any time: 1-800-448-3000

**Planned Parenthood** delivers vital reproductive health care, sex education, and information to millions of women, men, and young people worldwide: 1-800-230-7526

## THE QUESTION IS

Would you allow "a friend" to romance you into a questionable relationship?
The relationship leads to responsibilities that total 24 hours a day, 52 weeks a year
It lasts a lifetime

Payment arrangements, benefits, and shared duties rarely discussed
The friend may help occasionally, but you know more time and consistency is a must!
In time, "the friend" quits and is no longer around

And you now have all the responsibility for the commitment made
With many bills and worries that don't go away

The job is demanding and is different each day

You are now alone and learn volumes from the unbalanced relationship trade
You learn and become wiser in so many ways!

**Do you know?**

The US continues to have among the highest teen pregnancy, birth, and abortion rates in the developed world. [20]

Being raised by a single mother raises the risk of teen pregnancy, marrying with less than a high school degree, and forming a marriage where both partners have less than a high school degree.[21]

By: Mariyah Early

# BABIES
To Be or Not To Be

Babies are to be planned for, loved, and provided devoted care.

Babies are to be planned for, loved, and provided devoted care.

Babies are not to be had just because you're feeling low and want someone to love you.

Babies are not to be had just because you feel a baby will help you hold a man.

Babies are not to be had just because you're angry at the "other woman"

Babies are not to be had just because your friend has one

Babies are not to be had just because he tells you "lets have a baby"

Babies are not to be had just because you feel you are getting too old

Babies are not to be had just because you feel a baby will make you more responsible

Babies are not to be had just because you feel a baby will help him or you stop a drug habit.

Babies are not to be had just because you want to get even with someone.

Babies are not to be had just because you feel you need a tax deduction.

Babies are not to be had just because siblings want a brother or sister.

Babies are not to be had just because you break-up with him and find another who says "I love you—have my baby."

Babies are not to be had just to "trick him" into marriage.

Babies are not to be had just because you want a baby with "good looks and skin color like him"

Babies are not to be had just because you want someone adorable to play with and dress in cute clothes.

Babies are not to be had just because you're tired of going to school.

Babies are not to be had just because it's a glamorous, attention-seeking endeavor.

Babies are not to be had just because it's the only meaningful thing you think you can do.

Babies are to be planned for, loved, and provided devoted care.

Babies are to be planned for, loved, and provided devoted care.

*From Pain to Awakening: Evolving Into Women of Substance*

Tatiana E.

**Do you know?**

Each year, almost **750,000 U.S. women aged 15-19** become pregnant. **Two-thirds** of all teen pregnancies occur among **18-19 year olds.**[22]

# A CALL TO PARENTHOOD: A CALL TO RESPONSIBILITY

Talking to pregnant teens and women about pregnancy being a life altering decision
It's amazing the magical thought to this long-term commitment

When many become pregnant
Little thought or decision making occurs

The possibility of acquiring an STD is a totally different conversation
With the stakes much higher, depending on the STD and its violation

Most believe all will be fine

To inquire how the decision was made—
Logic, thought, and reasoning fades

"I don't know" — An easy answer!
"It just happened"
"I forgot to take my birth control"
"He doesn't like condoms"

"Will the baby's father be involved?"
Eyes roll upward—

"NOooo—Look at the scars on my body!"
"NOooo—He's in jail"
"NOooo—I don't have anything to do with him now."
"NOooo—He's going to help—I just don't know how!"
Wow!
Many parenting plans often conveyed:
"My parents will help"
"I guess there's no other way"

Boyfriends sit silent with little to say
Their silence fills the room
Their lack of maturity clearly resonates

Being there for moral support a noble gesture
The most important question they can answer
"Will you be there for your child's future?"

They are knights in glass armor
Visible, yet fragile to knowing the "man" it takes to be a father

Future grandparents with no voice in choices made
Is this thoughtless? Is this selfish? Is this responsible?
"What do you say?"

Scenes like this occur in many different places
Among different ages and races

Fathers there for conception
Leave soon with disappointing rejection!
Children left behind
Mothers blind to the pain that will unwind

## TALKING POINT QUESTIONS

How do you get to "know" someone?

Why is it important to "know" the person with whom you may have children?

Why is it important for girls and women to be in control of their sexual and reproductive health?

What causes some girls and women to allow boys and men to control their sexual and reproductive health?

What causes some girls and women to believe babies are problem solvers?

How can unplanned pregnancies affect your life?

# HAVE MY BABY

Some rappers rap about having babies and the glamour there
Believe their raps and you're going nowhere

Have a baby and let this logic rule
The risk is high you'll drop out of school

You want a house to be free
Chances are that won't be

The home you may can afford
Will have worn carpet and a broken door

Have a baby
Want a job
The money you earn will make you sob

Have a baby to give her the best
The responsibilities won't give you rest

Have a baby want to relax
You just don't know the facts!

Want a baby—Think it Out!
Weigh the consequences—Check it out!

Be in control of your Mind and Body
Or you'll be home changing diapers and bathing a little body
While he drops off diapers and goes with his boys to the next party!

## TALKING POINT QUESTIONS

Why is exercising good decision making a responsible self-management skill?

Why is it important to set goals for having children?

*From Pain to Awakening: Evolving Into Women of Substance*

## MY BABY'S DADDY

"My baby's Daddy"!

Why is he defined by a title and not a name?
Have you listened to this title game?
Is he more than fifteen minutes of fame?
Does he represent the title?
Or is what he's about really lame?
Have you considered why you don't say his name?
Why is he defined by a title and not a name?

## FIANCE

Your emotions betray what your words don't say
You worry if you talk commitment he'll walk away

You want him as a committed partner
You want your child to know him as father, husband, and be filled with pride

Not as your "fiancé" with his woman and all the trimmings on the side
Trust your feelings if this doesn't feel right inside
Your future does become what you decide!

**Do you know?**

Fatherless children are twice as likely to drop out of school. [23]

Children in father-absent homes are five times more likely to be poor.[23]

# ABSENT FATHER

It's Not About You
It's About Him

A father's love and presence is a valuable thing
A father not there for his child is truly insane
The absence of a father's presence causes untold pain
It leaves a child wondering—
"Am I to blame?"
It creates a troubled mind
And a heart requiring much love to not become cold and unkind

This is a message to boys and men who father children and disappear
Too immature to acknowledge the privileged gift of being a father

The betrayal and rejection your child will feel without you there
Will be like glass falling to the ground
Once whole—then fractured, the damage profound!

Your child will require a great amount of mother's love and explanation
Extended family's love and support for a long duration
A village of friends and mentors to heal the child's heavy heart & questioning mind

This message is to every child without an involved father
Always know and believe you're the best
Never settle for thinking less
You aren't responsible for your father's absence
Let no one make you believe less in yourself and place doubt in your mind
The reason your father isn't there is the answer he must search within to find
It's about him—Not you—Free your mind!

Let his absence not weaken or distract you
Or cause you to seek love in the wrong kinds of ways

Let's make it clear by saying it this way
Decide wisely about hanging with people who say they're your friends
Be a leader, not a follower, when they propose negative things

Know and believe trading your mind or body for someone's affection
Will not bring you love to replace the embrace your father's not there to give
Find strength in knowing there were many before you
Who have risen and not fallen without a father

Life begins as a challenge the day you are born
Let the challenges be a motivating thorn
It's how you respond and learn from obstacles that come your way
That will make you different and stand out from the rest
Or be complacent and settle for less

## TALKING POINT QUESTIONS

Are you responsible for your father's behavior?

Do you have to justify why he is not in your life?

What personal qualities do you need to have and/or develop to deal with his absence?

Can you "survive" and "overcome" without an involved father in your life?

*From Pain to Awakening: Evolving Into Women of Substance*

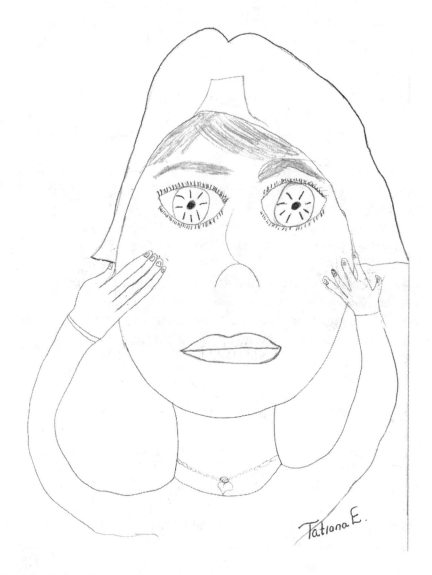

**Do you know?**

**Nearly half of pregnancies among American women are unintended**, and **4 in 10** of these **are terminated by abortion.** [24]

## DIFFICULT DECISIONS
Parent, Abort, Adopt

She wrestles with uncomfortable options
Overwhelmed by a recently discovered nine month reality
Constant worry affects her personality

Was it a choice, mistake, or accident?
It does matter
Many times feeling lost and alone
Her thoughts are all scattered

Critical decisions to make
Restless nights that keep her awake
Decisions to make are many
None you would envy

Through this troubled valley she walks
It's important she has wise counsel and unbiased talk

Hopefully in these objective conversations
True understanding comes from her concentration
For her mind to have a transformation
So the next journey will be untroubled and one she's ready to make


## TALKING POINT QUESTIONS.

What is the difference between choice, mistake, and accident?

Why is it important to use more than one safe sex practice and exercise personal responsibility when deciding to be sexually active?

*From Pain to Awakening: Evolving Into Women of Substance*

## YOUNG MOTHER IN TURMOIL

We spoke a little past nine
A young mother in jail for the first time

You may ask, "What was her crime?"
Somehow under her parental watch
Her infant died from her touch

She was consumed with guilt and confusion
Not totally understanding her emotional profusion

The baby, fussy and agitated
Took a last breath one dismal day

The details can read like a mystery novel
The crux of this story is the profound misery and sorrow

The most valuable piece from this tragedy you can take
Being a parent is the most serious decision you will ever make

It's more than buying cute baby clothes
It's more than playing with tiny toes

It's best to take the blindfold off your eyes
It's a decision that affects so many lives

Babies aren't little adults
They are totally dependent little ones

Their monotonous crying and need for 24 hour attention
Can lead to a tragic human collision
If you aren't aware of the things mentioned

True understanding of the parenting role
Can save so many who believe being a parent
Is a job they can have under control

Think beyond your limited thoughts and personal desires
Know that being a parent requires **love**, **commitment**, **planning**
And a great deal of **mature understanding**

**TALKING POINT QUESTIONS**

Why is it important to know the right reasons for having a child?

Why is it important to know the developmental characteristics and needs of infants and children before you have them?

Why is it important to know how to take "personal time outs" when stressed by infants and children?

**Do you know?**

Children in single parent families are more likely to get pregnant as teenagers than their peers who grow up in two parent families.[23]

Unmarried mothers are less likely to obtain prenatal care and more likely to have a low birth-weight baby. Researchers find that these negative effects persist even when they take into account factors, such as parental education, that often distinguish single-parent from two-parent families.[23]

Each day in America **2 mothers die in childbirth, 78 babies die before their first birthdays, 964 babies are born at low birth weight. 2060 babies are born without health insurance, and 2692 babies are born into poverty.** [25]

## HEALTH DISPARITIES RAP

Low birth weight babies
High infant mortality
When will we get in touch with reality?!

Compromised beginnings—short life spans
Statistics rattled off like nothing's said

Causes are many
We have to face
Forget about being defensive
Lives are at stake!

Let's confront them
Not wait!

Limited housing—crowded conditions
Neighborhoods troubled by unsafe traditions

Low income
Failed education

Inadequate finances
Raising an infant to an adult will take

Lack of prenatal care
Going to prenatal care too late
Missing too many appointment dates

Poor nutrition
Knowledge gaps—Folic Acid prevents birth defect traps

Diabetes, obesity, high blood pressure
Genetic disorders

Smoking
Drug use
Intimate Partner Violence
Teen births
STDs
Misunderstandings on whose sexual and reproductive life it is!

Stress and worry—causing many heartaches
Mothers tense, stressed, and afraid
This affects mothers and babies living on the edge

It happens locally
It happens internationally

We must wake up
Children deserve health, stable families, and a future

Another factor well studied and research based
Hard to confront
With a desire not to face

R — A — C — I — S — M research substantiates
Can be subtle, demeaning, brutal, often denied
For acknowledging it comes down to solutions to try
Confront it, take responsible action, with much persistence
Or
Put it back on a "shelf" and deny its existence

An easy escape
A weak defense
Racism as we know—Makes no sense!

It affects many lives
Causes stress
A contributor to infant mortality
Raises blood pressure—a medical reality
All these problems we must work to erase!

Communities can rise to a higher level of existence
Where children & families have optimum health and promising futures
We can do this!
Equality for all
It's Logical with Reason
Dismiss those who equate this to Anarchy and Treason!

## TALKING POINT QUESTIONS

Why is it important to have a preconception check-up?

Why is it important to receive early and regular prenatal care?

Why is it important to stop smoking when pregnant?

Why is it important to not drink alcohol or use illegal drugs while pregnant?

Why is it important to know the signs of preterm labor?

## CHILDREN COME FIRST
Not Last

When you have children and decide to date
Don't let misguided emotions put them last
And not first in the decisions you make

Your children come first
Relationships last
Don't let men enter your children's space too fast

Multiple entrances and exits affects so many lives
Your children were there before he arrived
And will be with you if the relationship dies

Children need responsible behavior to model
They require attention and good role models

Make certain you can do this with no bother
Show by your actions you are a responsible parent

And the mother in you is undeniably evident!


## TALKING POINT QUESTIONS

Why is it important to exercise good judgment when deciding to bring the man you date into your children's lives?

When is the most appropriate time to bring him into your children's lives?

What behavior from a male partner lets you know he shouldn't be in your life or your children's?

How do you safely work out a plan to leave the relationship?

What plan do you develop to not return to the relationship?

# BREASTFEEDING
The Gift

Breastfeeding is something I was asked to try
I turned my nose up and said—"WHY?!"

Having a baby so close and pulling on my breasts
It grossed me out!
It made me argue, "How can this be best?"

How can I feed a baby when I go to work, shop, or have someone to meet?
How will this work?
Who says this has to be?
I wasn't interested in this routine for me!

As you can tell
I didn't know it all
Even though I thought I did!
I've learned and now know
Breastfeeding is the most precious gift I could ever give!

## TALKING POINT QUESTIONS

What are your thoughts on breastfeeding?

Are you aware of the health benefits to the baby when breastfeed?

What reasons have you heard from women to not breastfeed?

**Do you know?**

How breastfeeding can benefit you and your baby?

**The LaLeche League provides excellent information, resources, and support on breastfeeding. http://www.llli.org/nb.html**[26]

*From Pain to Awakening: Evolving Into Women of Substance*

## BATTLEGROUND OR PEACEFUL COOPERATION
Children In The Middle

Parenting is a serious choice
With life often taking a circuitous course
From dating to marriage
To sometimes separation and divorce

There are key principles to keep in mind
When separation or divorce is the only solution to find
Some rules to follow and be first on your mind

Your child needs consistent contact with both parents to decrease feelings of rejection
Your child needs to feel confident there will always be love & protection

Your child needs all doubt removed the separation was because he or she was "bad"
Keep visits pleasant, cooperative, not sad

Relate as adults and not attack each other in the child's presence
Visits are about the child and not to check on the other parent

Refrain from power play tactics
Agree to be prompt at agreed visitation times

Agree to be consistent and fair with discipline
Agree not to place the child in the middle to carry messages or to confide
Agree to not use presents to have your child take a side

If you love your child
Let your child learn people can respectfully relate when they have differences
This will be a start in teaching your child to become a self-assured, confident person

## TALKING POINT QUESTIONS

Who are the winners, who are the losers, when children are in the middle?
Why is positive co-parenting important?
How do you define love, tolerance, peaceful co-existence?

# REVOLVING PAIN

# FRESH PAIN
Overcomer in the End

The stab of Fresh Pain
What do you do when it happens again?

What do you say when you thought it was at an end?
What do you do when things you thought were buried pop up again?
How do you cope when it happens again?
What do you say when it's front and center again?

How do you treat it when it sticks closer than a friend?
Why won't it leave and not trail you again?

What happens when you get close to your dream and stop—afraid to win?
What happens when shared secrets are released by the person you thought was your friend?

What do you do when those you thought learned the lesson do it again and again?
Why do you feel like a loser but know you're much better from within?

Why is Pain so arrogant and believes it will win?
Know your cup is bitter
But you're an Overcomer in the End
Know your Creator's sustaining presence is forever within
Seek it to forbid negative forces to win
You'll cry today and maybe tomorrow
But you will shed the Victim from within
You're an Overcomer from Beginning to End

*Surviving is a visible fight*
*Overcoming is an invisible peace*

# BLAME
A Senseless Game

What do you do when you run out of people and situations to blame?
And haven't sat with yourself to analyze your game!

What responsibility do you have to you
To analyze behavior and choices that get you "off course"?
When you don't listen to your inner voice!

Life has Pleasure
Life has Pain

You know how to prevent mishaps
But you keeping doing the same!

Blame will walk everywhere you lead
You have to sit with it
Allow it to rant and rave
Then conquer it
To make it go away!

## TALKING POINT QUESTIONS

How can blame get you off track?

Why is it important to confront your excuses?

How can this help you?

How can it change you?

From what sources can you seek help?

Why is it important to **listen** and be **open to new ways** to experience yourself differently?

## THE RANGE OF HURT
Intimate Partner Violence (IPV)

The Range of Hurt

The bruises and shame of intimate partner violence is an equal opportunity phenomenon. I have heard many tragic stories of abuse and witnessed the physical and emotional devastation it causes. I have worked with young girls and women with titles of teenager, student, resident, nurse, housekeeper, attorney, store manager, homemaker, substance abuser, incarcerated female, immigrant, and many other titles.
The hue of their skin tone varied from the whitest white to the darkest ebony. Their social class and financial status ran the spectrum.
They all were one, when it came to the depth of their hurt and the destruction to their inner selves.

Current statistics on Intimate Partner Violence, also known as Domestic Violence reveals:

On average more than **three women a day are murdered by their husbands or boyfriends** in the United States. In 2005, **1181** women were murdered by an intimate partner.[27]

In 2008, the Centers for Disease Control & Prevention published data collected in 2005 that **women experience two million injuries from intimate partner violence each year**. [27]

Nearly **1 in 4 women** in the United States reports experiencing violence by a current or former spouse or boyfriend at some point in her life.[27]

The United Nations Development Fund for Women estimates that at least **one of every three women globally** will be beaten, raped or otherwise abused during her lifetime. In most cases, the abuser is a member of her own family.[27]

**Give Yourself Permission:**

This makes it extremely important for girls and women to seek the help they need. To give themselves authority over their lives to leave relationships that endangers them or their children and strips them of dignity, respect, and self-worth.

**Do you know?**

The National Domestic Violence Hotline 1800-799-SAFE (7233)
1 800 787-3223 (TTY)
Anonymous and Confidential Help 24/7
www.theHotline.org[28]
Espanol
Ayuda anonima y confidencial 24/7

## DON'T BELIEVE THE HYPE

This poem is for girls and women who are in abusive relationships with boys and men. It also acknowledges women and men who are in same sex relationships and men who are in abusive relationships. Abuse to anyone, no matter the age and sexual orientation, is wrong and demoralizing.

Don't believe the hype
When he says, "You're nothing and just my type!"

He tells you his woman listens to his commands and knows to obey
She's under his control, and knows to stay

He says his woman has no mind
She deserves slaps and harsh words to keep her in line

A bruised lip, a scar on the face
You need this to keep you in place

He says, "You'll never make it."
He says, "You will never leave and will always take it"!

He says, "I'm your financial source."
"You can't leave, you have no choice, you have no voice!"

He sets the schedule for family and friends you can see
He says, "Go against this and be ready for the punishment you'll receive."

If any of this is a reflection of you
Choices must be made
Believe you have value
Seek the help to save you!

## TALKING POINT QUESTIONS

Why is it important to know the control strategies boys and men use to keep girls and women in abusive relationships?

Why is it important to be aware and not deny signs a love partner has anger control problems and other "red flag" warning signs?

Why are we more critical and blaming of a female who reports intimate partner violence?

Why are the obvious signs denied when boys and men exhibit bad behavior and girls and women believe "things will change or get better"?

How does a girl or woman's self-worth get trampled upon until she believes she isn't a person?

Why is the victim role one you can't assume?

What responsibility must you take to regain control in your life?

How do you safely develop a plan to leave the relationship?

What plan do you develop to not return to the abusive relationship?

# HOW COULD THIS HAPPEN
A Rising Star

Recognized in a popular women's magazine as a rising star
A distinguished career as a doctor on track and destined to go far

His profession the same with a planned, prestigious future
Beauty, Elegance, and Amazing intelligence she possessed
However, in a tragic quarrel
His life came to an end
Her life unraveled and began to descend

Her home entwined in yellow crime scene tape
Her life forever altered
What a cruel fate!

A misunderstanding and senseless dispute
Destroyed two promising lives no one can refute

Intimate Partner Violence excludes no social class
This is most tragic and not the last

If life events had magic to be placed in rewind and started anew
This would have been their wish and their families too!

*From Pain to Awakening: Evolving Into Women of Substance*

## HE TELLS HER—SHE OBEYS

She's 20
He's 18
He tells her what clothes to wear
And has the nerve to tell her how to style her hair!
He calls her disrespectful names that rhyme with "witch" and "more"
Her self-respect constantly stomped to the floor!

He keeps her on lock-down 24-7
She's afraid to go to the local 7-11

He stays out all night and says it's right
She questions this and it's an automatic fight

When he makes a sudden move
She feels, "Oh, No!" Another instance of his "manhood" he wants to prove!

She flinches with trembling fear of a blow
She knows he is ready and willing to throw

Sleeveless dresses she can't wear
Too ashamed to show bruises from his last terror flair

She's counseled and warned it will not get better
She ponders what's said, "Is it touching her grey matter?"!
She leaves with information and resources with her life at stake
The answer to her dilemma rests with the choices she will make

*From Pain to Awakening: Evolving Into Women of Substance*

## SHE'S INVISIBLE—TRYING TO FIND HERSELF

When I first met her she was quiet, sad, and wanted to die
A petite ebony woman with a tear in her eye

The pain and misery shown through like many I've seen
Hurt and cast aside by a life's journey that proved bitter and mean

I sat down with her and gave my full attention
Giving her respect—An often cast aside invention

Her eyes would dart from side to side
Weary that our eyes would suddenly collide

It was if she felt that her soul would completely drown
If we connected to each other on a higher ground

The shame she felt was ever so great
You wouldn't understand—How can I begin to relate?

I said I would never come to this jail no more
And here I am, a repeater, on the other side of the door!

My life has been one of drugs, violence, and gore
I just want to give up, I can't take it no more!

I thought I was strong and could stay away from crack
It pursued me relentless, I was weak, I gave up, I went back

I listened intently at the life she began to paint
Letting her know, I hear you, you have my attention, I'm a mere mortal, not a saint!

As she began to feel a little bit safe
Her defenses slowly began to erase

She began to tell about the heavy make-up she wore
She said it was camouflage to prevent the stares

I am in a relationship that's characterized by abuse
I tried to leave many times, I felt what's the use!

Our togetherness is a complex and chaotic thing
He beats me, loves me, yet I wait for his call
I know this is sick beyond belief
I can't figure it out, it gives me grief!

I've been in relationships by far much worse
I've been so hurt, I required a 24 hour nurse

One violent companion I tried to flee
Got me caught in a double paned window that trapped me

I was trying to jump from the window to flee his crap
The double paned glass became my trap

The glass cut viciously though my face and arms
I thought I was dead until I heard rescue alarms

My life has been like a dog chasing its tail
I want to succeed but many times fail

There are chapters in my life I can tell
I have covered them deep
They've been a living hell!

When I was young and didn't know much
A man I trusted held me in his tight clutch

He violated me
I carry the thoughts to this very day

I have fought the thoughts with alcohol, drugs, and many one night stands
I've been abused and hurt by many men's hands

You say I have purpose and I am much more than my past
Keep saying this, I want it to last

You say look in the mirror and say I am something
It will be hard, I feel I am nothing

You say with help and belief in myself
The disturbing thoughts aren't my future just part of my past

I am willing to take a step into the light
I am trusting with faith and help, I don't have to fear shadows at night
I am beginning to feel wrongs can possibly be made right

## HE'S ANGRY — I'M HURT

A few weeks ago she had a baby
Stressed and on edge — a distraught young lady

My fiancé has much anger
He frightens me
He feels like a stranger

He calls me names I'm ashamed to repeat
Curses and threatens to knock me off my feet!

He accuses me of sleeping around
His thoughts are irrational and not logically sound

His mood is up, his mood is down
His unpredictable behavior has made me flee
I'm staying with family until he is back to reality

"Can you give me a place he can go for counseling and medication?"
He says he will go
I think he's serious, but I really don't know

"How old is he?"
"He's 25 and a real live wire!"

If he's truly serious on making a change
His ability to call for help isn't out of his range

You say his mother wants to assist
She can sit by his side as he calls the list

Realize change will not be overnight
You and your baby deserve a future that is right
Not one filled with terror and fright

## ROTTWEILER
## THE CONVERSATION

A voice from afar frightened and stressed
I'm 20 years old and in a big mess

My dilemma is great
My fiance's dog is in the crate

He bit me once!
He is rambling and growling and moving so much
He is acting like he wants me for lunch!

I am pregnant and have a 1 year old
My fiancé knows the danger and treats us so cold!

He says his dog is here to stay
My pleas go unanswered—What else can I say?

Is there a safe place you can go?
The situation you are in is a definite no-no

I can go to my mom's home 75 miles away
I am very confused, I think I should stay

The danger to you and your child is too great
Your mom's home or a shelter is the best decision to make
Choose one, don't hesitate

I will, the stress is too great!

I don't want the dog to attack!
I must go—my fiancé is back!

Please call and let me know how you are?
She hangs up, a frantic voice from afar

*From Pain to Awakening: Evolving Into Women of Substance*

## COME BACK TO THE REAL YOU

He calls you the B—word and much more
Instead of laughing, "Show him the door!"
When did you decide this is the title you will claim?
Take responsibility—that's not your name!

Self-respect begins with you
Look in the mirror
Affirm every part of you!

Take off the people pleaser mask

Come          U
  Back        O
    To      Y
      The Real

By Mariyah

**Do you know?**

Dating relationships start younger than realized: nearly half of 11 to 14 year olds (tweens) have been in a dating relationship.[29]

Sex is considered part of tween dating relationships by a surprising number of tweens and parents—though parents believe it is not *their* tween who is having sex.[29]

Significant levels of abusive behavior are reported in tween dating relationships, and teens report that abusive behavior increases dramatically in the teen years (ages 15 to 18).[29]

Alarmingly, data reveals that *early sexual activity* appears to fuel dating violence and abuse among teenagers.[29]

Although most parents discuss relationships with their tweens, they really seem to be in the dark about what goes on.[29]

Today's tween relationship behavior may foreshadow a new wave of abuse among teens in the near future, unless something is done to prevent it. [29]

**Resources:**

www.thatsnotcool.com – A website for teens and parents on texting intimidation. **An excellent resource with great information and support.**[30]

**www.cdc.gov/chooserespectCenter for Disease Control's Choose Respect Initiative for teen violence prevention. Excellent information and resources.**[31]

## CONTROL

Control isn't a bad thing
It depends on how it's used and who goes on an ego ride
And transforms into Dr. Jekyll and Mr. Hyde

Control that is a maddening obsession
Can make the possessor obsessed
And make the possessed a distorted representative of the once confident self

Control of thoughts, actions, and words prevents hurt to occur
Self-control is a prized possession with invaluable lessons!

## THE PAIN

They came to meet as a couple
We began the process to define the trouble

After the initial conversation
She said, "I don't know if I want this relationship anymore".

We've been married for forty years
I have cried rivers of unseen tears

He abused me for many years
The last time has been over ten years

I know he is now a fairly decent man
My heart has grown cold, that's just how it stand

There is still pain deep inside
I can count on one hand the times I smiled as a bride

I am open and want to confide
I want to release the many hurts I've tried to hide

I see the hurt you carry on your face
It will take time but you'll come to a better place

I began to see hope in her worried face

**Do you know?**

Today's older woman has been in an abusive relationship for many years[32]:

She grew up in an era when divorce was frowned upon.[32]

She may split family solidarity (by wanting to leave the abusive relationship).[32]

She's become resigned to a pattern of living that has gone on for decades.[32]

## TO MY SISTERS
With Sincerity and No Play

If I could be transformed for a moment into a repentant man, this is what I would say to all girls and women who have been physically and emotionally hurt by any male.

To my sisters
Words have power
The magnitude of their importance is critical when searching for the right ones to say
However, I'm truly at a loss today!
This expression of regret is sincere with no play

I apologize for any man or boy who has hurt you in any way
You did not deserve to be pushed, hit, shoved, threatened, intimidated, shamed,
disrespected, and made to believe this is love
This behavior is from a coward and not representative of a man!
My deepest regret and apology
With sincerity and no play!

# SEXUALLY TRANSMITTED DISEASES

༄

**CHLAMYDIA HIV/AIDS PID(PELVIC INFLAMMATORY DISEASE) GONORRHEA**

**SYPHILIS TRICHOMONIASIS HPV (GENITAL WARTS)**

**HERPES HEPATITIS VAGINITIS CRABS (PUBIC LICE)**

**Do you know?**

**Resources:**

National STD Hotline 1800 227-8922 (Herpes, Chlamydia, and other infections)

AIDs National Hotline (CDC) 1 800 232-4636

Teen Helpline 1 800 400-0900

The Gay and Lesbian National Hotline: Peer Counseling, information, and referrals

1 888 THE-GNLH (1 888 843-4564)

Herpes Resource Center 1 800 230-6039

**Do you know?**

Girls and women 15-19 years old had the largest number of reported cases of chlamydia in 2009 of any age group. Females are at greater risk of acquiring infection, and the consequences include pelvic inflammatory disease, pregnancy complications, and infertility. [33]

The HIV rate was 7 times greater among Blacks than Whites in 2006. [34]

Young adults and teens, under the age of 30, continue to be at risk, with those between the ages of 13 and 29 accounting for 34% of new HIV infections in 2006, the largest share of any age group.[34]

*From Pain to Awakening: Evolving Into Women of Substance*

*From Pain to Awakening: Evolving Into Women of Substance*

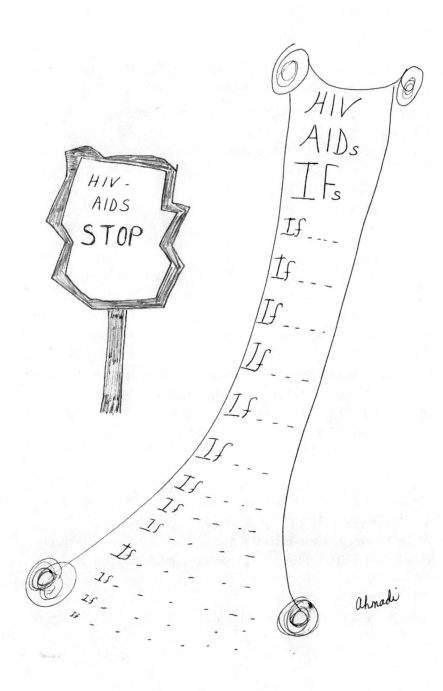

## HIV/AIDS
The Real Deal

HIV/AIDs
7 Short Letters
With BIG consequences and LITTLE understanding

Let's know the right information!

HIV is the Infection
AIDs is the disease

You can't get HIV by sitting next to someone
Shaking hands, giving a hug or dry kissing
Using restrooms, water coolers, or telephones
Eating in a restaurant or cafeteria
Swimming in a pool or using hot tubs
Being bitten by an insect or donating blood

HIV is transmitted thru unprotected sex and its many techniques
You can get it by sharing needles and syringes with an HIV+ person
By exposure to HIV before or during birth
Or by breastfeeding

AIDs is the most serious type of HIV infection
It results from the destruction of the infected person's immune system
It destroys the body's T-helper white blood cells
White blood cells are the cells in your body that fight infections
This leaves an HIV infected person vulnerable to many diseases

This is a brief review
Read & learn more about it to protect you!

## HIV/AIDs
### Ifs

IF you think looking at someone can identify their HIV/AIDs status
YOU'RE WRONG!

Don't go by this unreliable test
That's true MADNESS!

IF you think people will tell you they are infected
That's UNAWARENESS!

IF you think an intimate partner is truthful when told
"You're the only one!"
Or
There were only "a few" before you and they were "OK"
Good ego boosters, without question!
However, allow your mind to have reasonable doubt for your protection!
Ask them to get tested
Or
Show you their HIV test results

The same proof is required of you
Protect yourself with safe sex—if you want a future!

IF you're scared to test to know your status
Living in fear is disastrous

The unknown places your life on a roller coaster ride
Testing is a difficult decision to make
Waiting and guessing prolongs your headache

Find the courage to take the test
It's better to know, than to guess!

## ITCHES — IT BURNS

She came to clinic after rushing through traffic
Quite talkative, and most graphic

It's burning and itching down there
The pain I'm in is a real nightmare

I can't stand, walk, or sit without pain
I went to see one doctor
I moaned so much — he thought I was an actor!

He said it looked like gonorrhea!
Flashbacks occurred to the casual partners I regretted!

I just want this pain to stop!
How do I pay for medication?

My finances are low
She looked somewhat hesitant

I was told one is $50 bucks
This mess I'm in truly sucks!

Upon further examination, a lesser infection was the cause of her discomfort
No gonorrhea, the welcomed report
She breathed a sigh of relief

Remember to take care of your health and practice safe sex!
You may not be as lucky the next time around!

She confirmed with strong conviction as she was homeward bound
"Please believe me — I WILL!

The risks are too high — You best be for real!

## TALKING POINT QUESTIONS

Why is it critical to your physical and mental health to practice safe sex?

Why is it important to be in control of your sexual and reproductive health?

What do you do to be in control of your sexual/reproductive health?

What do you do to maintain good sexual/reproductive health?

# VIOLATED
# SEXUAL ABUSE

**Do you know?**

**Resources:**

Rape, Abuse, Incest, National Network (**RAINN**) 1 800 656-4673

Stop It Now (Sexual Abuse) www.stopitnow.org[35]

Stop It Now 1 888-PREVENT Call on Thursdays EST 12-4pm to speak to someone

Child Help USA 24 Hour Help Line 1800 422-4453

National Child Abuse Hotline 1 800 4ACHILD (1 800 422-2443)

National Runaway Hotline 1 800-621-4000 or 1 800 RUN-AWAY (1 800 786-2929)

Child Welfare League of America (CWLA)

Is an association of nearly 1000 public and private nonprofit agencies that assist over 3.5 million abused and neglected children and their families each year with a wide range of services.

www.cwla.org[36] National Headquarters Arlington, Va. 703 412-2400

**Do you know?**

Child sexual abuse is reported almost 90,000 times a year. It is estimated that 1 in 4 girls and 1 in 6 boys is sexually abused before 18 years of age.[37]

# TOUCHED

If you have been touched in a most inappropriate way
It's important to find someone to hear what you have to say

I know it's difficult, you want to keep it hidden deep
The mixture of thoughts causes you restless sleep

You believe somehow the fault points to you
Please BELIEVE this isn't true

Search and find the strength from within
To remain silent keeps secrets buried
And the wrong person wins

## TALKING POINT QUESTIONS

Although difficult, why is it important to have courage to tell someone you trust about your sexual abuse?

Why is it important to have the abuser be accountable for his or her actions?

Why is it important to you?

Why are we more critical and questioning of a female who reports sexual assault?

Why do we assign a different set of values/beliefs on who is credible, the female or the male?

*From Pain to Awakening: Evolving Into Women of Substance*

By Mariyah

## BELIEVE OR BETRAY
Do The Right Thing

When your child, no matter the sex or age
Confides in you he or she has been sexually molested or abused
LISTEN!
Don't dismiss it
Act to protect
Not to blame

This painful sharing is more times truth than a lie
Search within, if your first response is—
"That's a lie!"

When secrets are revealed to the one thought the right one to tell
Several things can happen or be destined to fail

You can listen
Provide emotional support
Act to protect
Or—
Freeze, because this is a part of your past you don't want to relive or reveal
Deny, because taking action will "Disrupt your life"
Of all the choices
Belief, Protection, Investigation, and Action are the right ones to make
An act of betrayal is the hardest for a child to take

## INTO THE CLOSET
The Questioning

Into the Closet we walked
She said for a short talk
What did you do?
What did you say?
When you talked in court today

Did they ask what he did
Timidly I said, "Yes, they did."
Repeating silently within
"I hope this questioning will soon send"!

The relationship we were in
Made me uncomfortable and know she wasn't a friend
Soon it was over
As though it never began
Back in my seat
Thoughts circling within
And thankful it had come to an end!

# VIOLATED
Why?

Why do we make the "Violated" the persecuted ones?
Who have to prove all that was done
And disbelieve the "Victimizer" could be the one!

# DIVERSITY

## What is a hate crime?

Hate Crime: A Definition from http://www.stophate.us/hcpa.html[38]

A crime in which the defendant intentionally selects a victim because of the actual or perceived race, color, national origin, ethnicity, gender expression or identity, disability, or sexual orientation of any person.

## Resources:

Hate Crimes Prevention Center 1629 K St NW Wash DC 20006

http://civilrights.org/lcef/hate/toc.html[39]

Hate Watch **monitors hate groups on the internet** http://www.hatewatch.org[40]

Anti-Defamation League **monitors Hate Groups** http://www.adl.org[41]

KlanWatch, a **project of the** Southern Poverty Law Center, **monitors the activities of racist and neo-Nazi groups throughout the United States** http://www.spicenter.org/intelligenceproject/ip-index.html[42]

National Asian Pacific American Legal Consortium **documents hate crimes against Asian/Pacific Americans** http://www.ncl.org/anr/partners/napalc.html[43]

NAACP A National organization for ethnic minorities in US www.NAACP.org[44]

National Headquarters Baltimore, MD 877-NAACP-98

LAMBDA Legal is a national organization committed to achieving full recognition of the civil rights of lesbians, gay men, bisexuals, transgender people and those with HIV through impact legislation, education and public policy work. www.lambdalegal.org[45]

**Do you know?**

In 2009, Hate crime statistics reported: 61.1 percent of all hate crimes were committed against persons, while 38.1 percent were crimes against property. Of the 4,057 victims of racial bias, 71.5 percent were victims because of an offender's prejudice against blacks. Of the 1,575 victims of anti-religious hate crimes, 71.9 percent were victims because of an offender's anti-Jewish bias. 31.3 percent of hate crime incidents happened in or near the victim's home. 17.2 percent took place on highways, roads, alleys, or streets. [46]

# DIFFERENCES
Its Many Human Elements

Time has rhythm without end
It changes days into months
Months into years
And years into decades

There are some things elusive to time that is out of its domain
Certain human feelings and behaviors remain constant with slow change

Fear
Harassment
Discrimination
Stigmatization
Victimization

Are human frailties that continue to exist and exert unimaginable stress and pain
Why homophobia, racism, sexism, classism, and other isms continue to exist is a perplexing matter

If you are human and a bit inquisitive
You can dialogue in your mind people and situations you don't understand

No matter the degree of your understanding or knowledge deficit
Rude remarks
Open Contempt
Or entertaining physical threat or emotional harm to someone you don't like or understand
Whether they are gay, bi-sexual, transgender, a different race, religion or culture is out of the question!
We have to check our thoughts, responses, and actions throughout our life

With the complexity of national and international problems that shadow our life
Individual conscious thought on how we treat each other
Should come first and not always last

When we can acknowledge differences
Commit to live our lives with tolerance to eliminate hate and discrimination
Our humanity will elevate to a higher level of peaceful co-existence

## TALKING POINT QUESTIONS

Why is it important to be knowledgeable of racial, sexual, religious, cultural and other differences of people with whom you will have interaction?

How comfortable are you socializing with someone of a different race?

How comfortable are you working with someone of a different race?

When you meet someone from a different race, do you see their color first or do you see them as a person first?

Do you believe the various shades of one's skin color plays a part in how one is accepted or excluded by their racial group or by another racial group?

How often do you think about your race in your daily interactions at school, work, social gatherings, and other social exchanges where you are the minority, where you are the majority?

What needs to occur for skin color to not be considered in how we relate within our racial group and how we relate to others outside of our racial group?

Why is it important to eliminate hate and discrimination?

# From Pain to Awakening: Evolving Into Women of Substance

## THE GREAT RACIAL DIVIDE

Children the color of Vanilla Chocolate and Hershey Bars
Biased by skin color and how it speaks to the value of who they are!
Light Chocolate, Milk Chocolate & Hershey Bars disbelieving
they're beautiful and Superstars!
White Mint believing Light, Bright, and Oh So White
Is the standard of what's Good and Right!

Bottled up self-rejection can dim the soul's inner light
It's like being knocked out in Round One of a Ten Round Fight!
It speaks to what is wrong and needs to be made right!

How can we send rockets into space?
And have children withdraw from each other
Because of the color of their face

Where did this start?
When very young they were color blind
With no idea how color is perceived in the mind!
This is so asinine!
If this were a crime
Think how many would serve time!
What would be the recidivism rate?
For daily practicing—discrimination and hate!

Condemn you forever like the three strikes and you're out policy
A criminal's worst fate!

When children psychologically tested proved it
Why do we continue to exclude by color
And stand with pride to sing the Star Spangled Banner!
Are we the Land of the Free and Home of the Brave?
Or are our minds more imprisoned
Than Mandela cast aside on an island far away!

The Great Racial Divide
Why is it widening
Is the answer—color dividing?

**Do you know?**

The CNN program analyzing White and Black children's bias towards lighter skin.[47]

*From Pain to Awakening: Evolving Into Women of Substance*

# SUICIDE

∽

*S*ometimes at your most desperate moment you can think life isn't worth living.
Before you do something to harm yourself, please call someone you trust to talk out your worries.

**Resources:**

**If you are in crisis and need help right away please call your local 911 Emergency Service or Suicide Prevention 24 Hour Hotline: 1 800 SUICIDE** 1800 784-2433 or **The National Suicide Prevention Lifeline, a service available to anyone. You may call for yourself or for someone you care about. All calls are confidential. 1 800-273-TALK 1 800 273-8225**

**Do you know?**

Suicide is a major, preventable public health problem. In 2006 it was the leading cause of death in the U.S., accounting for 33,000 deaths. It was the third leading death for young people ages 15 to 24. It was the seventh leading cause of death for males and the sixteenth leading cause of death for females.[48]

Risk factors for nonfatal suicide attempts by adults include depression and other mental disorders, alcohol and other substance abuse and separation or divorce. Risk factors for attempted suicide by youth include depression, alcohol or other drug use disorder, physical or sexual abuse, and disruptive behavior.[48]

A 2009 survey of more than 7,000 lesbian, gay, bisexual, and transgender (LGBT) middle and high school students (aged 13-21) found that in the past year, because of their sexual orientation—**eight in ten** had been verbally harassed at school, **four in ten** had been physically harassed at school, **six in ten** felt unsafe at school, and **one in five** had been the victim of a physical assault at school.[49]

# A FATHER AND MOTHER
## No More

A father and mother to two
Came in a code, placed on life support, his face pale blue
He was homeless and depressed by bureaucratic rules to carry him through
Disturbed by his rambling life as he tried to take care of himself and the two
He thought placing a gun to his head the only thing to do

The grief to the family left behind
May have been the first and last thing on his mind

Many times we're unaware of the problems others carry
Whether it's being homeless, distressed, or having multiples hurts and much worry

The lesson from this sorrowful event
Be aware of those around you
Do your best to have a listening ear without a hurried rush
Some time to understand
And a helpful gesture whenever you can


## TALKING POINT QUESTIONS

Why is it important to seek professional help and other support with problems that affect you?

What makes people reluctant to seek help for emotional pain and more willing to seek help for physical pain?

Why is it important to understand that both are equally important and require the same emphasis and timely response for treatment?

Why is it important to have **compassion and empathy** as part of your character?

*From Pain to Awakening: Evolving Into Women of Substance*

# HOMELESSNESS

**Do you know?**

**Homelessness Resource:**

National Coalition for the Homeless: 1012 14th St. NW Washington DC Suite 600 Wash, D.C. 20005 202 737-6444

National Runaway Hotline 800 621-4000 or 1 800 RUN AWAY (1 800 786-2929)

**Do you know?**

—A study by the National Law Center on Homelessness and Poverty states that approximately 3.5 million people, 1.35 million of them children, are likely to experience homelessness in a given year (National Law Center on Homelessness and Poverty, 2007). [50]

On an average night in 23 US cities surveyed, 94 percent of people living on the streets were single adults, 4 percent were part of families and 2 percent were unaccompanied minors. Seventy percent of those in emergency shelters were single adults, 29 percent were part of families and 1 percent were unaccompanied minors. [50]

Due to the recent foreclosures crisis, homelessness has been on the rise. In the U.S. Conference of Mayor's 2008 Report, 12 of the 25 cities surveyed reported an increase in homelessness due to foreclosures and another six didn't have enough data to be sure. Thirteen of these cities had adopted policies to deal with the recent increase in displaced citizens of the housing crisis, but 10 cities had not implemented new policies. [50]

# NO WHERE TO GO

The faces of the homeless are a mosaic of many disrupted lives
People existing—barely getting by

Some too proud or too scared to accept a shelter bed
Or they find there is no shelter to be had

Affordable housing is becoming more and more out of reach
It causes many to make their homes shelters and side streets
The homeless are—

The incarcerated woman released from jail on a cold winter's night
No money or bus fare to any destination site
Tempted to commit a petty crime to return to jail
Knowing this to be a reliable haven without fail

The teenager who finds the streets more peaceful and less threatening
than a chaotic home life

The mother with children, tired of living from family to friends
She lives in a shelter developing a plan to make the cycle end

The amputee who wheels around the street at night until the morning light

The teenager who relocates to a new area to escape the past
Suddenly recruited into a wayward life to make her money last

The mentally compromised woman who has burned family bridges
Now pushes a grocery cart with her belongings up and down the street

The HIV+ man whose family shuns him and provides no space on their floor
Scared of a disease they don't understand
He's not welcome at their door

The woman whose husband leaves her and his children
She can't afford to keep the home
Can you imagine the pressure she's feeling?

Working class families displaced from their homes by "neighborhood revitalization":
Tricky words for "neighborhood extermination" and "family disintegration"

Families made homeless by deceit and greed
Homes foreclosed and now in desperate need

Veterans wander down the street
They have served their country well
And now need to be "well-served" by their country
They must go through mounds of "red tape"
The madness of this is hard to take

The dialysis patient who leaves treatment to live under a bridge in a cardboard tent
Many people shun him because of his scent
The drug addicted HIV+ woman who trades her body for a $10 crack rock
The buyer unaware of her health status and thinks safe sex is a "crock"
The teenager who lives hidden between homes until his cover is blown
The faces of the homeless are these individuals and more
Ones you pass but don't really see

## TALKING POINT QUESTIONS

What are your thoughts on this social problem?

Why do you think it exists?

What recommendations do you have to solve homelessness?

# SUBSTANCE ABUSE

Do you know help for substance use and abuse?

Resources:

**underagedrinking.samhsa.com**
**abovetheinfluence.com**

AL ANON and ALA TEEN

1 800 4AL-ANON (1 888 425-2666)

Cocaine Anonymous National Referral Line 1 800 347-8998

Narcotics Anonymous 1 818 773-9999 Hours: Mon-Fri 8am-5pm Pacific Time

Pride Institute: 1 800 547-7433 Hours: 24 hours a day, 7 days a week

Chemical dependency/mental health referral and information hotline for gay, lesbian, bisexual, and transgender community.

**Drug Alcohol Treatment referral National Hotline:**
1- 800- 662-4357

**Do you know?**

Binge drinking typically happens when men consume 5 or more drinks, and when women consume 4 or more drinks, in about 2 hours. [51]

Although college students commonly binge drink, 70% of binge drinking episodes involve adults age 26 years and older. [51]

About 90 % of the alcohol consumed by youth under the age of 21 in the U.S. is in the form of binge drinks. [51]

The proportion of current drinkers that binge is highest in the 18 to 20 year old group (51%).[51]

## A SEMESTER LOADED

She thinks she's together and Oh so Chic!
She can carry 18 semester hours, and drink malt liquor to the "wee hours"
She feels it's quite bold to tell
"I can down 2 six packs, have fun, and not fail!"

She wipes away hangovers in her apartment tower
With multiple showers by the hour
Friends and family know her frivolous comments
And try relentless to prevent her descent

They know eventually she'll crash
And talk to her with determined pleas
"You have a future you're making your past!"

It's sad but hopelessly true
The only one who can save her from herself
Is her
Not the many "you's"!


## TALKING POINT QUESTIONS

Why is it important to be knowledgeable about alcohol and drugs and the affect they can have on your body, mind, and entire life?

Why is it important to exercise judgment and personal responsibility when you are invited to use drugs or alcohol?

Why is it crucial to be a leader and not a follower when offered choices that can negatively impact your entire life?

Why is it important to seek treatment to end substance abuse and addiction?

Why is it important to give up people, places, and things that negatively impact your life?

Why is it important to write personal goals and objectives to stop drug use? (with professional assistance)

Why is it important to write a relapse prevention plan before completing treatment? (with professional assistance)

## CRACKHEAD

Crackhead is what I'm called
I cringe when people laugh, joke, and use that name
It makes me so ashamed!

I know the fault lies with choices I've made
I don't like using crack and being afraid

It's something I thought I'd never do
It hurts each time I come to jail
I don't like living in alleys with police on my trail

I despise the things I did for a $10 rock
Scared of who might hurt me at the next block
It's dangerous out there and hell in here
I will be clean—free from fear—not chasing a rock
I won't run to another crack house in the dark

I owe this to myself, my children, and my mother
I can no longer make so many suffer

I pray & commit to get my life together
I've buried the shame, and reclaim "my" name
You count me a loser—but I'm not the same!

## BE REAL FOR YOU
Not Me

She says a bit smug
Everyone knows marijuana isn't a drug!

I laugh and sometimes sigh
At the false reality of this try

She continues on to say
"David and I usually have a few joints a day"

We don't smoke around the children
It mellows me out
It helps him to think clear and squashes doubt!

It doesn't make you paranoid
Stop! Listen! Did you hear that noise?

I do my best work when I've had a joint
I know what you're thinking! I'm for real! It's not a joke! Get my point!

I can do many things at once — You know, multi-task
I'm sorry, What did you just ask?

Did I tell you we're raising our children to be vegetarians
We can't just let anything contaminate their bodies
Like processed food, pork, and neighborhood junkfood parties

If it is one thing we are
Its health conscious

She makes more illogical comparisons
The contradictions to what she says is beyond her reach
She never contemplates what she will nonsensically preach

She defends marijuana and is "always" right
Debating her is a useless fight!

Criticizing some food choices has merit
However, some other comparisons have no credit

My comeback to her non-stop chorus
Be Real for You—Not Me—Is All I Ask

# WOMEN IN VARIOUS STORMS

**Mentoring Resources:**

**National Cares Mentoring Program** is dedicated to recruiting and connecting mentors with local youth serving and mentoring organizations to help guide struggling Black children to academic and social success and to close the gap between the relatively few Black mentors and millions of vulnerable youth. **Susan Taylor, Founder, and Former Editor-in-Chief, Essence Magazine. Contact:** 1 888-990-IMIN (4646) http://www.caresmentoring.org[52]

**Boys and Girls Clubs:** Are located in all 50 states, Puerto Rico, the Virgin Islands and on U.S. military installations around the world. http://bgca.org/Pages/index.aspx[53]

Go to their website enter your zip code for the one near you.

**Big Brothers and Big Sisters:** A National Mentoring Program for boys and girls.

http://www.bbbs.org[54]Go to their website enter your zip code for the one near you.

**Do you know?**

Children from single parent families are more likely to be in trouble with the law than their peers who grow up in two parent families.[23]

## MAMAS BOYS

I have experienced some interesting phenomena
And well played out melodrama
Working with men and women behind locked doors
What proved quite perplexing were the older "mamas boys"
Grown men 18 plus and mothers 40 and more
Calling to see when sons would walk thru the door

Many still making excuses for their sons incorrigible behavior
And quick to make snap assessments about their names on the jail roster

They said, "It must be a flaw in the legal system."
True for some, but not for many

Interestingly enough
Men outnumbered women in the "worried mamas" calls

The litany of their requests proved to be quite a list
Let me tell you some of what it did consist

Is he alright?
Does he sleep well at night?
Does he have money for commissary?
Will he be released the first of January?
Can you tell him I will visit and not worry?

How do you reframe the "Inquiring minds want to know question?:
"How do you continue to pamper a grown man this way?"

This has to be a teaching moment for all women rearing sons alone
Search out every resource and support you can
To help you parent a boy into a responsible man
If you know you have done all you can
And he doesn't see value in being an upright man

*From Pain to Awakening: Evolving Into Women of Substance*

You have done an admirable job
Be at peace—Don't sob!


**TALKING POINT QUESTIONS**

Why is it important for mothers (and fathers) to instill in their sons from childhood to adulthood to have respect for themselves, respect for girls and women, and personal responsibility for the choices they make?

Why is it important for single mothers to seek male support from trusted family members, friends, and community programs to help mentor their sons?

Why is it important for single mothers to rear their sons (and daughters), according to their developmental age, to be independent and assume responsibility for their actions?

Why is it important to instill in children to seek parental support for daily life challenges they need information and support (example: bullying, sex education, etc.)?

## A TRIP TO THE EMERGENCY ROOM

One mother clothed in fear
Sat beside her son in an ER chair
With a syncopated accent
She worried out loud about her son's facial "accident"
As she spoke, several older children nodded in agreement

My son was jumped as he walked home from school
He wasn't aware of their presence with the Ipod in his ear

They grabbed and beat him close to home
He was so frightened, and all alone
What causes children to be so mean?

Words are difficult to provide an answer
For there are no good ones to explain the absurdity of violence

A respectful attempt made to decrease her anxiety
All the while knowing
Another mother would come to the E.R. with the same difficult question

She left wondering, "Do I keep him at home or send him to school tomorrow?"
What will happen this week and the ones to follow?
"I can't afford to move, I can't stop working."
"I feel like screaming, I just want to holler!"

Women today, whether in large cities or small towns
Are united with one common cause:
Keeping their children safe
Whether it is from gang bangers, drug dealers, child predators, or terrorist threats

Vigilance, inner strength, spirituality, and constant prioritizing
Become keys to their never ending strategizing

Frequent calls home for safety checks
To quiet the throbbing in their chests

Moving anxiously home through rush hour traffic
Not totally reassured until home and there is nothing tragic

What a daily test!
An emotional stress

Knowing they can't carry this burden alone
They release this anguish to their spiritual power
To provide strength to manage life hour by hour

**Do you know?**

Students who are bullied may fear going to school, using the bathroom, and riding on the bus.[55]

# A MOTHER'S PAIN

Sitting with a woman who has lost her child
Whether it's to illness, abduction, or a car going 90 miles an hour
These unexplainable situations can turn average days into infinite dark hours

Hurt runs deep and emotions run wild
For she knows her heart is torn and her mind is on fire
She thinks, Oh God, this can't be true
This most unconceivable occurrence is so strange
It's like a bad dream, with scenes that don't change

She wants to open her eyes and find this is a cruel joke
When cool tears glide down her face shocking her into reality
She comes to a numb awakening
Truth is sometimes difficult to take
It's something the mind can't conceal
As she gathers her thoughts and absorbs what is surreal

She knows her belief in a higher power
Will sustain her through the darkest hours
In time she will channel this pain so raw at the surface into purpose

**Do you know?**

In a study by the U.S. Department of Justice:

797,500 children younger than 18 were missing each year, or an average of 2,000 children reported missing each day. [56]

203,900 children were abducted by family members[56]

58,200 were abducted by non-family members.[56]

**Resources:**

For Missing Children: 1 800 THE LOST 1 800 843-5678

National Hotline for Missing and Exploited Children: 1 800 843-5678

**TALKING POINT QUESTIONS**

How important is it to have a spiritual connection to sustain you in difficult times as well as good times?

Why is it important to find a way to channel individual pain into purpose?

What have you learned about yourself when you have been in difficult situations?

**Do you know?**

The nation's prisons held approximately 744,200 fathers and 65,600 mothers at midyear 2007.[57]

## GUARDED DELIVERY
Emotional Pain
Far Greater Than The Physical Pain

Shackled and in Labor
To the hospital she comes to deliver her baby
Under different circumstances this would be a cherished time
No words adequate to express her elation
This birth is far from ideal
For her human connection will be two guards — her 24 hour protection

The bitter-sweet reality of nurturing her child will be 24 to 48 hours at best
A quick return to a small cell without the baby once warm at her breast
No preparation can ease the pain or quiet the panic in her chest

No matter the time to exchange for the crime committed
The separation from her child will be the hardest and most regretted

## TALKING POINT QUESTIONS

Why is it important to seek professional help for past "hurts" that still affect you?

Why is it important to end behaviors that can entrap you in the legal system?

Why is it important to you, your children, and other people close to you?

Why is it important to give up people, places, and things that can negatively impact your life?

Why is it important to develop a lifestyle plan to prevent re-incarceration? (with professional assistance).

# TROUBLE

I know trouble will come
The difference will be how I will allow it to stay
It will come with arrogance and the threat to destroy
I will confront it
And let it know it's a challenge—not a threat
A mere inconvenience at best
I will let it know I've had similar visitors before
Health struggles, financial problems, misunderstanding from family, friends, and more
I've entertained each for a minute and then shown Trouble the door

## TALKING POINT QUESTION

Why is it important to know that life will have problems and opportunities and each has their lessons?

# ROAD SIGN WISDOM

These road signs are metaphors to the challenges we confront in life

Bumpy Road — Life will have challenges

Follow Signs — Be Coachable

Stay in Your Lane — Keep focused

Road Narrows — Life isn't predictable

Decrease Speed — Slow down, see where you are, and where you want to go

Proceed with Caution — Know where you detoured, Reclaim your destiny

Exit traffic construction — You will make it thru

## TALKING POINT QUESTION

Why is it important to refer to these signs when life becomes challenging?

## I FEEL GOOD ABOUT ME
It Starts When You're Young, Can't You See

I feel good about me
It starts when you're young—Can't you see!
I love myself
I believe in me
I love myself unconditionally!
No one can take my self-confidence
My life has unknown potentiality!
I am learning to make the right choices for me
I don't let Drama accompany me!
I feel good about me
It starts when you're young—Can't you see!

## TALKING POINT QUESTIONS

Why is it important for mothers and fathers, grandparents and others to talk to girls from the womb through adulthood that they are important, loved, and worthy of respect?

Why is it important to teach them to think of the pros and cons of choices they will make?

Why is it important for fathers to show their daughters love, tell them they love them, and be an integral part of their lives?

# RESPECT

A soulful diva said it best
All I am asking for is a little RESPECT!

You may think this is too much to ask
Believe in yourself
And know it's an accomplishable task

Respect begins with self
If you don't have it for you
You will not receive it from anyone else

If you have baggage you carry
Take out each piece that makes you weary

Look critically within
Sort out stumbling blocks that have cluttered your path
Deal with each one that has caused your wrath

If you can't go through each bag without fearing the unknown
Know you don't have to go it alone

The essence of what this is saying
Once there is no delaying
A different reassured self you will be portraying

## FREE

When I set my mind free
I began to see the good in me

Self-doubt was removed
Self-assurance became my reality

My life has substance
A most profound revelation

I listen to myself
I'm not guided by false friends

I don't respond to their telephone rings
I place their calls on re-direct
Much of what they've said has been quite suspect

I know I'm judged by the company I keep
I've learned
Lost time makes you weep!

I stayed with "friends" many unproductive hours
My intuition whispered, "This is not a good decision!"
I'm now free from inhibitions
I look forward, not back

If I could grant you gifts with the greatest worth
I would anoint you with clear vision
Consecrate your mind with invaluable wisdom
So that when you reach a fork in the road
You will know the one to lead you in the right direction
And the one not to go for your protection!

# RESURRECTION

I've come to my Resurrection
Not looking for false Protection
I know I am a marvelous Creation
This is my Confession

I see a new me on the horizon
Deserving the right kind of love
One not characterized by mistreatment and unrequited love

I thought I was beyond deserved love
I'm wiser from help above

I walk with confidence, character, and dignity
This is my identity

I'm glad they came sooner than later
My head is on straight

Forgiveness has come
I've buried the hate

I know freedom from the one who caused me pain
I know that person is the weaker one
My soul is free, it's not on the run


My awareness comes from above
I'm grateful for my Creator's unfailing Love

## FORGIVENESS

Forgiveness is like a house built without a quality roof
To make it "complete" to prevent inside damage
A solid roof has to cover the house
Instead of making a reliable roof
A builder can decide to look for old tiles and roof fixtures
He knows immediately where to find these roof covers
He has gone to the same sources before
They are easy to obtain with little effort

Instead of getting substantial fixtures that will prevent long-term damage
The builder uses old fixtures that offer a "temporary fix"

So it is with the cruelest hurts we have experienced
Whether it has been physical, emotional, verbal, or sexual abuse
These hurts can be continually patched with anger, not letting go, and reliving the past

The abuses can't be taken lightly
They MUST be worked through with the right help
Take however long needed to come to a place of healing & forgiveness
And when you have reached this place
Release the one from your mind who has caused you pain for you to truly live again

For the random mean acts towards you
Ones that are thoughtless, angry, and vindictive
Entertain them for less than a minute
Offer a prayer and send them on their way
You may never know the answer
Or understand why people say and do the things they do

If you hold on to grief and distress they have no problem to give
You will emotionally sink and they will be the winner

If you do determine why they did what they did
What do you do with the answer
Do you decide to have anger and contempt
Or decide they have occupied too much of your life and let go

Moving forward means exactly that
Staying in known hurt
Gives power to the one who hurt you

Again, the most severe hurt requires professional help
And time to reach an acceptable point of forgiveness

The everyday hurt that stings like a bad paper cut
Requires immediate dismissal from your life

## COMING OF AGE

Know as a woman you have come of age
Ready to live with a strong desire to turn the page
Not afraid to step forward on any stage

You're inspired with grains of wisdom
That fills you with determination to surpass your greatest ambition

You take on challenges without hesitation
To rearrange what you need to turn your life's pages

You hush quiet storms within
To experience you so different there is no emotional emptiness

You walk with determined insistence
It lets people know
You have substance, no matter your experience

They look at a woman who has a glow
They know it's not a pretense show

They see something has occurred that makes you who you are
You have a radiant countenance
It's a look that denotes confidence & grace
You don't settle for commonplace

It tells them you are refreshing, inspiring, and different!

You hold your head high and reflect you are three times a lady
You are a woman who can walk on any stage
In your company, you are worth true homage!

## COCOON

My mind has unwrapped like a butterfly from a tight cocoon
Striving to live right
To not be uptight

Shaking off dreams that have gone wrong
Knowing there's a lesson in every sad song
Committed to be strong

Living for today
Anticipating tomorrow

Understanding you can have joy today
And at night be wrapped in unimaginable sorrow

Rejoicing through it all
Knowing when I stumble
I will get up from the fall!

Remembering the past
Thanking God it moves and doesn't last!

Moving forward
I'm in a race
You'll lose if you try to match my pace!

I've got somewhere to go!
I can't move slow

I've set my course
Decided my choice

I'm in it to stay
If you're not in it to win it
Get out of my way!

## TALKING POINT QUESTIONS

Why is it important to stay focused?

Why is it important to set goals?

Why is it important to believe you can win?

Why is it important to "not beat yourself up" if you get off track?

Why is it important to learn from your detour and get back on track?

Are you in it to win it?

## THE RACE

I'm in a race with time
If I get sidetracked
It will leave me behind
Then I'll have to restart
How can this be smart?
To have the advantage and be misguided
Like a robot with wires crossed
And have to be reprogrammed to get back where I stopped!
To see the finish line in the distance
And become stuck by a lack of persistence!
Time keeps moving
It has a destination
It won't wait on me
It won't wait for you
It won't wait for anyone to decide
Do I run this race?
Or do I let life pass me by!


## TALKING POINT QUESTIONS

Why is personal empowerment priceless?

Why is it important to love yourself first?

Why is it important to respect yourself first?

Why is it important to be an independent thinker?

Why is it important to be a leader not a follower?

# WOMEN OF SUBSTANCE

## WOMEN OF SUBSTANCE

Some you know by their wealth and fame
Millions of others don't have that recognition to claim

A Woman of Substance
Evolves from birth
There's no way to measure the value of her worth

You won't know her by her trials
For she hides them in unmarked files

You won't know her by her Treasures
For she counts them as Blessings
And can walk away from what gives her Pleasure

You won't know her as the center of attention
She feels the focus on her doesn't need to be mentioned

How will you know a Woman of Substance?
She will be someone you meet

Smart, Proud, and not necessarily stand out in a Crowd
Wise by mistakes made

Remembers her past as a learning path that started her on her way
It defines who she is and what she has to say

She's young
She's old
She has a story to be told

Who is she?
She's you
She's me

Still Learning
Transforming
Non-Conforming
Still more to be!

Quiet
Shy
Shaken by past hurts
And still willing to try

She's shed tears
She's conquered fears

She's fallen
She's risen

Her Spirit is Free
With a Mind not Imprisoned

## TALKING POINT QUESTIONS

How would you define a Woman of Substance (WOS)?

What qualities does she have?

How do you work towards being a Woman of Substance?

What "life quick sand" can get in your way of being a WOS?

How do you know when you become a WOS?

How do you maintain being a WOS?

## WEAVE SOME MAGIC

I want to weave some magic
I want to make lives less tragic
I want to move girls and women to respect their God-given temple
To love, affirm, and know their body is a temple!
To be responsible for their body and mind

Yes! I want to weave some magic
To have girls and women refuse to be puppets to false attractions
And get caught up in misguided actions!
I want girls and women to be **Offended** when they're wanted for their **Behind**
And not wanted for their **Mind!**
Yes! I want to weave some magic!

I want to use the words I say
To make someone stop and not be led astray!
To totally commit this is a new day!
To crawl, walk, run, and get away
To prevent inner decay!
To take responsible action and not be afraid to say:
I won't be a pawn of anyone!
I won't be tempted by taunting dares!
I won't take thoughtless actions that lead nowhere!
I won't spiral down!
I won't have my dreams drown!
I denounce that life and won't claim that throne!

Yes! I want to weave some magic!
To cause girls and women to think
And be responsible for their actions!

## GRANDMOTHERS, GRANDFATHERS, AUNTIES, SISTERS, AND MORE

Grandmothers, grandfathers, aunties, sisters, and more
Parenting 1st, 2nd, and 3rd generations as they walk thru their door

Bound by values to take care of their own
They can't turn their backs and say—"Leave me alone!"

Juggling health, financial, and social conditions
They do what is within their power to parent their family's children

They manage and do their best
They know there is little time to be depressed

They stand in for relatives not there to parent
Or ones who lack awareness that their absence or "visible" presence
Now have relatives accepting responsibilities that are unending

Grandmothers, grandfathers, aunties, sisters, and more—their love is transcending!

### TALKING POINT QUESTIONS

Where would families be without the concern of these family members who step in and parent children in their family? (rhetorical question)

What commits them to take on this responsibility?

What must occur within families for some parents to accept responsibility for themselves and their children and not pass it on to other relatives?

**Do you know?**

Since 1990, the number of children living in households maintained by grandparents has increased 30%. In 2000, 5.8 million grandparents were living with one or more grandchildren. Of these, 2.4 million grandparents were solely responsible for meeting the basic food, shelter, and clothing needs of their grandchildren.[58]

They keep families together when parents are unable to care for their children due to factors such as drug abuse, child abuse and neglect, poverty, incarceration, or mental and physical illness including HIV/AIDs. [58]

# SINGLE MOTHER
## A Title, Not A Stigma

Let's not place all single mothers in a one size fits all basket
There are many different single mothers
Ones who are responsible, loving parents
Concerned about their children's interest

They work with great determination to provide their best
They may accept a "temporary safety net" of government assistance
And not rely on this for lifetime financial assurance
Many are able to persevere without this option as their economic defense

There are single mothers who work jobs that aren't strictly 9 to 5
Check on their children consistently
And make the best care arrangements available and do it with pride

They prepare meals, check homework
Juggle work schedules to attend school meetings and special events
Launder clothes
Wash, style, and cut hair
Run to their children's room to calm a nightmare

Give baths to the younger ones
Monitor the hygiene of their teens
Check to see if grace is said before meals
Run to the pharmacy to doctor cold chills
Stand at the bedroom door to ensure nightly prayers are fulfilled

Manage a tight budget that rivals many Wall Street bankers
Laugh and playfully tease
And know when to be strict to provide the discipline their children need

They instill in their children spiritual reverence
They let them know they are loved

And that with work, faith, and determination
They can surpass their greatest ambition

## TALKING POINT QUESTIONS

Are you surprised by the positive statistics on single mothers?

What causes single mothers to be "labeled"?

Do you know any single mothers who are responsible parents?

What characteristics do they have that you admire?

**Do you know?**

In 2008, there were 9,753,000 single parent families with children under 18 maintained by mothers or 84.1%. 70.7% of these mothers were employed.[59]

# BOLD AND CLASSY

I'm Bold and Classy
Driven and Sassy
I know me, and know me best
I can look you straight in both eyes
Laugh and not trip by your cruel lies

My body is a temple
Don't offer me drugs, you must be simple!

You say what? Let's have a baby?
My head is on straight—I decide that, you must be crazy!

I don't hesitate and will walk away from anyone
Who disrespects me and tries to make me feel I'm no one

I decide my choices!
I'm smart, I listen to wise and experienced voices

You laugh and joke about females who think you are worth a fight
One day they will find self-respect and know that's not right

You say it's not good to have a spiritual source
ENOUGH IS ENOUGH!

One day you will bow down and ask for forgiveness in a trembling voice
From
    That
        Spiritual
           Source!

## TALKING POINT QUESTION

Why is it important for girls and women to be **"direct"** in letting boys and men know what they will and won't tolerate in their lives?

## MY SISTER FRIENDS
## MY TRUE FRIENDS

It's amazing how we talk for hours on an array of events
Talk several days later and have more to say
It's so good to have you there
To discuss funny life situations and know I can let down my hair

It's freedom to know my confidences I can share
And that you will listen and keep it there

Your wise counsel and a desire to listen is cherished
Because I appreciate that you—REALLY LISTEN!

You know how to challenge me when I get off course
I treasure you because you're my prized support source

If there were more women friends like you
To help see each other through
IMAGINE the magnitude of collective and individual power
That would make the strong stronger
And the weak more empowered!

**TALKING POINT QUESTIONS**

Why is the friendship and support of "sister friends" a cherished gift?

Why is it important for women to hold information shared with them in confidence?

# GRANDMOTHERS
Special women beyond Belief

Grandmothers watch over their grandchildren who are their most special gift
They shower them with love and pray for their protection
They give them uncompromising affection
They encourage them to be principled and move cautiously in the right direction
Grandmothers are wise with tons of experience
They know their challenges and when to come to their defense
They feel the need to hold them close
They know their grandchildren have to walk singularly in the world each day
They send up many prayers to bless them on their way

They are not always aware of what their grandchildren may face
But know they will be surrounded by God's grace
Grandmothers provide instruction in confidence, pride, and determination
They instill ethics, faith, and moral direction
Praying these will be their defense
When their grandchildren are approached with lots of nonsense

Grandmothers pray they will hold true to their moral values
And make the right decisions
They rely on their grandchildren to remember their wise voices
When the world challenges them to make wrong choices


## TALKING POINT QUESTIONS

What qualities have impressed you with grandmothers you have known?

Why is it important to model these qualities and pass them down from one generation to the next?

*From Pain to Awakening: Evolving Into Women of Substance*

# Becoming An Empowered Woman

## Behavior Prevention/Change: A Model for Self- Empowerment

~

**What Is It?**

It is a self-empowerment model that can be used individually, in a support group, one-on-one with a counselor, or one-on-one with a family member, friend, or other support source. It comprises a pre and post self-assessment and a Behavior Prevention/Change Plan which guides a girl or woman through a plan to prevent or change behaviors of concern.

**What can it do?**

The **pre and post self-assessment** can be used as a reference point for self-evaluation by girls and women. The self-assessment can be taken prior to reading the book and several months after reading to re- assess for changes in thinking and behaviors. The last section of the assessment can be used after reading each theme to become more aware of information presented. It can guide an individual to contemplate making an identified lifestyle change needed for personal empowerment.

It is helpful to use the self-assessment in combination with reading the range of empowerment poetry in the areas of female identity and self-worth, real-life family dynamics, health, and spirituality. The various poetry themes have talking point questions to encourage critical thinking on the various day-to-day life situations that are part of our lives. The questions are intended to be echoes of conscious thought we all must engage in to assess our personal life challenges and act in a responsible manner to resolve. The **do you know** questions provide relevant statistics to validate the various themes, and the **resources** provide relevant toll-free numbers, information, and support sources in areas of personal need and concern. The vivid illustrations are both comical and serious to illicit thinking and discussion.

The **Behavior Plan** includes personal affirmations, understanding the **stages of change** to address behavior challenges, and the usefulness of developing **SMART Goals** (Specific,

**M**easurable, **A**chievable, **R**ealistic, **T**ime-Framed) to initiate **Action** on personal behaviors of concern to the individual.

## A Personal Note to Counselors

*The author has used this model in a women's empowerment group she conducts entitled "Women of Substance". The group is held at a city jail in central Virginia. The Model and content of the empowerment poetry can be used for various individuals and groups (mentoring groups, group homes, residential treatment centers, schools, church groups, and similar sources). The various poetry themes can be used in session and for homework. Motivational Interviewing and the Stages of Change by Dr. Carlo C. DiClemente are incorporated in the women's group.*

*The women have responded with enthusiasm and look forward to participate in each week's theme topic. We role play, develop individual affirmations, weekly present each group member's affirmation, listen to music, view and discuss video clips specific to theme topics, develop and present individual self-empowerment collages at the termination of each group, and much more. It is inspiring to see each woman begin to experience herself in a new way and become open to make lifestyle changes to become more **informed and empowered**.*

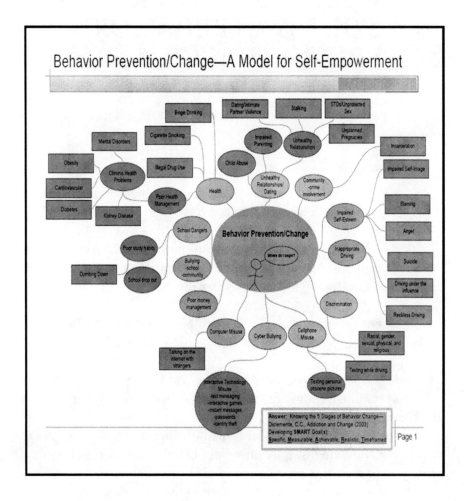

# UTILIZING EMPOWERMENT POETRY IN BEHAVIOR PREVENTION/CHANGE

સ્ર

1. It's important to be perceptive to recognize your **potential** to engage in behaviors that can have negative consequences.

2. It's also important to be **aware** of current behaviors you are engaging in that are potentially self-destructive and can lead to long-term negative consequences.

To identify some of these behaviors, please refer to the Behavior Prevention/Change: A Model for Self-Empowerment.

To begin to work on behavior lifestyle changes; the range of poetry, illustrations, facts, resources, and talking point questions are excellent "jump off points" to read, reflect, and discuss with someone you trust (family, mentor, professional counselor). This is the beginning of preventing or changing behaviors that concerns you or concerns someone who cares about you.

For **high risk** areas, i.e., substance abuse, intimate partner violence, bullying, and other similar areas, it's also important to discuss these concerns with someone you trust as noted above.

Counselors trained in Motivational Interviewing (MI) will be good facilitators to help you with change because in MI the individual is seen as the one who can bring about change for him or herself due to an intrinsic motivational desire to change the behavior. The counselor does not dictate change.

The counselor works with the individual thru simple, yet specific steps that respects the person and guides the person thru their plan of change for themselves. It's not magic, however, if a person is willing work on their plan of change, change can occur.

3. The next step is to think positive and believe you can forego engaging in behaviors with negative consequences.

4. Next, complete the Woman of Substance Self-Assessment on how you feel about yourself and your concerns. From the Self-Assessment and Model, identify behaviors you want to begin to work on.

5. To begin your process for change; it's important to daily think positive and surround yourself with positive thoughts and people, varied social activities, prayer, meditation, assertive behavior, and other positive ways to let your feelings and desires known and understood.

To understand and appreciate the challenges and rewards of working on making positive changes, the Stages of Change by Dr. Carlo C. DiClemente is a good reference for understanding the Process of Change. The model sets forth 5 stages that persons go through towards making change.[60]

# WOMEN OF SUBSTANCE

## PRE AND POST SELF-ASSESSMENT

*Please indicate the test type by shading the appropriate bubble.* O Pre-Test or O Post-Test

*Instructions: Completely shade the bubble that best describes your feelings.*

| *Please rate your feelings on the following statements:* | Agree | Unsure | Disagree |
|---|---|---|---|
| I feel good about myself. | O | O | O |
| I feel that I am a failure. | O | O | O |
| I appreciate and feel confident about who I am. | O | O | O |
| I feel unappreciated at times. | O | O | O |
| I look forward to the future. | O | O | O |
| I do not expect to get what I want. | O | O | O |
| I feel good about my appearance. | O | O | O |
| I have someone to talk to about personal problems. | O | O | O |

| | | | |
|---|---|---|---|
| I have someone to give me help with a problem. | O | O | O |
| I feel confident expressing myself to make my needs known. | O | O | O |
| I respect diversity (racial, cultural, religious, sexual differences). | O | O | O |
| Wise money management is important to me. | O | O | O |
| Learning & improving my education is important to me. | O | O | O |
| I am pro-active in managing my health (wellness check-ups, managing chronic health conditions, etc.) | O | O | O |
| I express anger appropriately. | O | O | O |
| I make responsible decisions to be in healthy relationships | O | O | O |
| I respect myself. | O | O | O |
| *Please rate your feelings on the following statements:* | Agree | Unsure | Disagree |
| **I take responsibility and precautions to prevent sexually transmitted diseases to myself and others.** | O | O | O |
| I take precautions to prevent unplanned pregnancies. | O | O | O |
| At times, parenting my children can be challenging (if applicable). | O | O | O |
| *When I face a stressful event or problem:* | Agree | Unsure | Disagree |
| I try to keep busy or act like it didn't happen. | O | O | O |
| I put my trust in a spiritual source. | O | O | O |

| | | | |
|---|---|---|---|
| I tell my feelings to someone. | O | O | O |
| I use alcohol or drugs to make me feel better. | O | O | O |
| I just give up trying to reach my goal. | O | O | O |

**One or several things I've began to think about or I am more aware of to help improve myself in this counseling session or thru reading a specific theme in this book is:**

# STAGES OF CHANGE:

## PRE-CONTEMPLATION

*The state in which there is little or no consideration of change of the current pattern of behavior in the foreseeable future.*

**Tasks:** Increase awareness of need for change; increase concern about the current pattern of behavior; envision possibility of change.

**Goal:** Serious consideration of change for this behavior.

## CONTEMPLATION

*The stage wherein the individual examines the current pattern of behavior and the potential for change in a risk—reward analysis.*

**Tasks:** Analysis of the pros and cons of the current behavior pattern and of the costs and benefits of change. Decision-making.

**Goal:** A considered evaluation that leads to a decision to change.

## PREPARATION

*The stage in which the individual makes a commitment to take action to change the behavior pattern and develops a plan and strategy for change.*

**Tasks:** Increasing commitment and creating a change plan.

**Goal:** An action plan to be implemented in the near term.

## ACTION

*The stage in which the individual implements the plan and takes steps to change the current behavior pattern and to begin creating a new behavior pattern.*

**Tasks:** Implementing strategies for change; revising plan as needed; sustaining commitment in face of difficulties.

**Goal:** Successful action for changing current pattern. A new pattern of behavior established for a significant period of time (3-6 months).

## MAINTENANCE

*The stage wherein the new behavior pattern is sustained for an extended period of time and is consolidated into the lifestyle of the individual.*

**Tasks:** Sustaining change over time and across a wide range of different situations. Integrating the behavior into the person's life. Avoiding slips and relapse back to the old pattern of behavior.

**Goal:** Long-term sustained change of the old pattern and establishment of a new pattern of behavior.

## HOW READY ARE YOU FOR CHANGE?

On the scale below, with **0** being the least ready to **10** being the most ready, circle where you are on the scale of being ready to make a behavior change for yourself.

**0    1    2    3    4    5    6    7    8    9    10**

**Least**                                                                 **Most**

You now have a reference point of where you are on readiness for change. It is now your task to make a decision to begin the work of change. If you're not ready, and change is important to you, think about what's causing you to be stuck. A professional counselor can work with you on helping you to identify why you are "stuck" and work with you to move forward.

## GROUNDING YOURSELF:

*Affirmations:*

Affirmations are words or phrases said consistently to affirm positive feelings and beliefs about you or other people. They are needed to daily combat negative thoughts that can cause you to be negative and pessimistic. It speaks true to the saying, if you think you can you will AND if you think you can't you won't!

## STEP 1

Let's write a positive self-affirmation for you. Using the first letters in your name, write your personal affirmation. For example: My name is **Ahmadi.**

| | |
|---|---|
| A | Aware that my life has unknown possibilities |
| H | Having faith that I can be all that I want to be |
| M | More than eager to do all within my power to make my dreams come true |

**A**    As I look forward to every opportunity to improve myself
**D**    Dedicated to loving myself in good and bad times
**I**     I know I can make changes in my life to better me!

Read consistently your affirmations and write additional ones for yourself. Keep a positive attitude to deflect the negativity that you will daily face.

## STEP 2

Take the following 4 actions towards your Behavior Change, after identifying a behavior you want to change:

**Example: I want to lose weight.**

| ACTION 1 | ACTION 2 | ACTION 3 | ACTION 4 |
|---|---|---|---|
| **LIST POSITIVE CHANGES** | **ACKNOWLEDGE CHALLENGES TO CHANGE** | **SEEK RESOURCES** | **WHAT EACH WILL DO** |
| I will feel good about myself. | The majority of the people in my family love to eat and have weight issues. | Healthcare provider<br><br>Peer support group | Monitor my weight loss program.<br><br>Challenge me to maintain diet. |
| I will prevent chronic health problems. | It will be difficult to change my eating habits. | Healthcare provider | Annual physicals.<br><br>Health education/ support |
| I will be able to participate in activities w/o becoming short of breath. | I don't like to walk. | Community Wellness Programs | Health programs<br><br>Community Recreation<br><br>Wellness buddies |

| | | | |
|---|---|---|---|
| I will be able to wear the clothes that I like. | I've become used to wearing baggy clothes. | Talk to friends who have lost weight | Clothing Suggestions<br><br>Peer Support |

## STEP 3

Write behavior goals to address the behaviors you want to correct. For example, your SMART GOAL for weight loss could be to: **Prevent/Stop Poor Health Management**

**Your SMART GOAL(Specific, Measurable, Attainable, Realistic, & Time-Framed Objectives) could be:**

1. I will lose 30 lbs. to be within my ideal body weight of 150 lbs by July 30. I will:

    a. Schedule a medical appointment with my MD on March 10 to develop a weight loss plan.
    b. I will lose 2 lbs. each week.
    c. I will daily follow the recommended diet.
    d. I will walk 30 minutes 5 days a week.
    e. I will reward myself with something special when I lose the first 5 lbs.

## FINALLY!

Be consistent with your work on your plan. Also realize that you may slip and get off track. Just remember what you have already learned, how far you have come, and it won't be as difficult returning to your goals. Believe in yourself and know that you own the responsibility to make the changes to improve your life.

# REFERENCES

[1]Real Girls Real Pressure: A National Report on Self-Esteem (2008) http://www.dove.us/#/makeadifference/report.aspx (accessed February 8, 2011)

[2]http://www.girlshealth.gov (accessed January 31, 2011)

[3] http://www.healthyteennetwork.org/ (accessed February 10, 2011)

[4] Limber, S.P. (2002) Addressing Youth Bullying Behaviors. Proceedings from the American Medical Association Educational Forum on Adolescent Health: Youth Bullying. Chicago, IL: American Medical Association. http://www.ama-assn.org/amal/pub/upload/mm/39/ (accessed January 26, 2011)

[5]T. R. Nansel et al., "Bullying Behaviors Among U.S. Youth: Prevalence and Association with Psychosocial Adjustment, Journal of the American Medical Association 285, no. 16:2094-2100

[6]http://www.merriam-webster.com/dictionary/compassion (accessed February 10, 2011)

[7]gethelp@nvc.org (accessed February 10, 2011)

[8]stopbullyingnow.hrsa.gov/kids (accessed February 10, 2011)

[9] www.bully.org (accessed February 10, 2011)

[10] http://www.practicalmoneyskills.com/personalfinances/creditdebt (accessed February 9, 2011)

[11] Alliance for Excellent Education, Issue Brief (August 2009) http://www.all4ed.org/publication_material/issue_policy_briefs?page=1 (accessed February 1, 2011

[12] Alliance for Excellent Education, Issue Brief (April 2010) http://www.all4ed.org/publication_material/issue_policy_briefs?page=1

[13] http://www.cdc.gov/obesity/data/index.html (accessed February 15, 2011)

[14] http://www.cdc.gov/heartdisease/behavior.html (accessed February 15, 2011)

[15] http://www.cdc.gov/HealthyYouth/obesity/ (accessed February 15, 2011)

[16] Hartocollis, Anemona (5 June 2010). "Growing Obesity Increases Perils of Childbearing" (http://www.nytimes.com/2010/06/06/health/06obese.html?th&emc=th)The New York Times (accessed February 9, 2011)

[17] http://www.alz.org/documents_custom/report_alzfactsfigures2010.pdf (accessed February 14, 2011)

[18] http://www.alz.org/national/documents/report.africanamericans-silentepidemic.pdf (accessed February 21, 2011)

[19] A Randomized Controlled Trial on Effects of Transcendental Meditation Program in Blood Pressure, Psychological Distress, and Coping in Young Adults http://www.ncbi.nlm.nih.gov/pubmed/19798037 (accessed February 10, 2011)

[20] http://www.kff.org/womenshealth/upload/3040-05.pdf (accessed February 7, 2011)

[21] Teachman, Jay D. "The Childhood Living Arrangements of Children and the Characteristics of their Marriages." Journal of Family Issues 25 (January 2004):86-111.

[22] www.gutmacher.org/pubs/FB-ATSRH.html (accessed January 26, 2011)

[23] http://www.fathers.com/content/index.php?option=com_content&task=view&id=391 (accessed February 10, 2011)

[24] http://www.guttmacher.org/pubs/fb_induced_abortion.html (accessed January 26, 2011)

[25] http://www.childrensdefense.org/child-research-data-publications/each-day-in-america.html (accessed January 26, 2011)

[26] http://www.llli.org/nb.html (accessed February 15, 2011)

[27] http://endabuse.org/content/action_center/detail/754 (accessed January 26, 2011)

[28] http://www.thehotline.org (accessed January 26, 2011)

[29] Tween and Teen Dating Violence and Abuse Study. February 2008. Teen Research Unlimited (TRU,2008). Liz Claiborne Inc. Tween Relationship Study

[30] http:///www.thatsnotcool.com (accessed February 15, 2011)

[31] http://www.cdc.gov/chooserespect/ (accessed February 15, 2011)

[32] http://www.musc.edu/vawprevention/research/olderbattered.shtml (accessed January 11, 2011)

[33] http://www.kff.org/womenshealth/upload/3040-05.pdf (accessed January 26, 2011)

[34] http://www.kff.org/hivaids/upload/3029-11.pdf (accessed February 1, 2011)

[35] http://www.stopitnow.org (accessed February 22, 2011)

[36] http://www.cwla.org (accessed February 22, 2011)

[37] http://www.ncvc.org/ncvc/main.aspx?dbName=DocumentViewer&DocumentID=32315 (accessed February 22, 2011)

[38] http://www.stophate.us/hcpa.html (accessed February 22, 2011)

[39] http://civilrights.org/lcef/hate/toc.html (accessed February 22, 2011)

[40] http://www.hatewatch.org (accessed February 22, 2011)

[41] http://www.adl.org (accessed February 22, 2011)

[42] http://www.spicecenter.org/intelligenceproject/ip-index.html (accessed February 22, 2011)

[43] http://www.ncl.org/anr/partners/napalc.html (accessed February 22, 2011)

[44] http://www.NAACP.org (accessed February 22, 2011)

[45] http://lambdalegal.org (accessed February 22, 2011)

[46] http://www.fbi.gov/news/stories/2010/november/hate_112210/hate_112210 (accessed February 22, 2011)

[47] http://www.cnn.com/2010/US/05/19/doll.study.reactions/index.html (accessed February 9, 2011)

[48] http://www.nimh.nih.gov/health/publications/suicide-in-the-us-statistics-and-prevention/.index.shtml (accessed February 25, 2010)

[49] http://www.cdc.gov/lgbthealth/youth.htm (accessed February 11, 2011)

[50] http://www.nationalhomeless.org/factsheets/How_Many.html (accessed January 26, 2011)

[51] http://www.cdc.gov/alcohol/fact-sheets/binge-drinking.htm (accessed February 7, 2011)

[52] http://www.caresmentoring.org (accessed February 6, 2011)

[53] http://bgca.org/Pages/index.aspx (accessed February 6, 2011)

[54] http://www.bbbs.org (accessed February 6, 2011)

[55] National Education Association (2003). *National Bullying Awareness Campaign*.www.neaorg/schoolsafety/bullying.html (accessed January 26, 2011)

[56] http://www.missingkids.com (accessed January 21, 2011)

[57] http://bjs.ojp.usdoj.gov/index.cfm?ty=pbdetail&iid=823 (accessed February 22, 2011)

[58] http://www.aecf.org/~/media/Pubs/Topics/Child%20Welfare%20Permanence/Foster%20Care/HelpingGrandparentsRaiseGrandchildrenWhoSucce/grandparents.pdf (accessed February 11, 2011)

[59] http://www.catalyst.org/publication/252/working-parents (accessed February 11, 2011)

[60] Diclemente.C.C. Addiction and Change (2003) p. 27 Copyright Guilford Press. Reprinted with permission of The Guilford Press.